Learning Team Facilitator Handbook

A Resource for Collaborative
Study of *Classroom Assessment*
for *Student Learning*

Jan Chappuis

Educational Testing Service
Portland, Oregon ■ Princeton, New Jersey

Cover design: George Barrett

Book design and typesetting: Curtis Bay and Heidi Bay, Grey Sky Design

Editing: Robert L. Marcum, editorbob.com

Project coordination: Barbara Fankhauser

Educational Testing Service
317 SW Alder Street, Suite 1200
Portland, OR, 97204.

Printed in the U.S.A.

ISBN 978-0-8868538-8-4

Library of Congress Pre-assigned Control Number (PNC): 2007933233

Acknowledgements

Learning Team Facilitator Handbook is the product of the knowledge and skills of many people. Teachers, administrators, and staff developers who have conducted learning teams with CASL program materials have graciously shared their insights about what makes learning teams work, what causes them to fade out, and what stops them cold. Their observations have informed the bulk of the suggestions you will read.

Over the past six years, my colleagues Judy Arter, Steve Chappuis, Rick Stiggins, and I have wanted to create a more robust support product for learning teams. We have long discussed and planned out what it might contain. This handbook owes a great deal to their knowledge of and commitment to learner-centered adult professional development.

Creating a coherent text from multiple documents and idea sources is a technical writing challenge, one that I would not have attempted alone. Robert Marcum, freelance production editor, has tirelessly worked to perfect the mechanics and the flow of ideas. Design consultants Heidi and Curtis Bay have developed the layout and color scheme to communicate meaning with simplicity, precision, and elegance on each page. Barbara Fankhauser, communications director in the ETS Portland office, has shepherded the production process. Much credit for clarity is due to this team.

Perry Loveridge and his team at Picture This Productions devised the set and provided the direction for the *Handbook* DVD. Perry's talents as set designer, director, and producer have guided us through the creation of all interactive training videos that comprise the CASL program. I am especially thankful for his patience and his vision.

And finally, our cheerful and competent office staff—Mindy Dotson, Ivona Kiebasinski, and Jennifer Cavanagh—have assisted with myriad details, from tracking down permissions to proofreading.

I am grateful to all of you for your dedication, perseverance, and generosity.

Jan Chappuis
Portland, OR
July 2007

Table of Contents

List of Figures

Tab 3 Leading and Managing the Learning Team Experience

no figures in Tab 3

Tab 4 Resources for Learning Team Members

Tab 5 Additional CASL Program Resources

Learning Team Facilitator Handbook DVD Contents

1

Introduction

Purpose	To give an overview of the goals and content of *Classroom Assessment* for *Student Learning: Doing It Right—Using It Well*; to describe the content of the *Learning Team Facilitator Handbook DVD* and how to use it; to explain the learning team concept and process
Content	◆ Purpose of the handbook ◆ How to use this handbook ◆ Goals of the CASL program ◆ Learning Team Facilitator Handbook DVD: Program and Chapter Introductions ◆ Features of the CASL text ◆ Our model for professional development in classroom assessment competencies ◆ Introducing the concept of learning teams to others

1 Introduction

Purpose of the Handbook

CASL Text

We have designed the *Learning Team Facilitator Handbook* so that you can more successfully conduct learning teams around the study of the text *Classroom Assessment* for *Student Learning: Doing It Right—Using It Well* (which we refer to throughout as *CASL*).

Built into the *CASL* text are lots of ideas and activities for maximizing learning about classroom assessment; *CASL* is your first best friend in developing assessment expertise. This handbook is your second best friend. It's designed to help you get learning teams started and keep them going without the need to rely on an outside expert. The contents have been chosen specifically to help anybody be a better planner, leader, and manager of the learning team experience. You may not use everything in this handbook, but you should be familiar with its contents, so you can use them in either a planned and structured or an ad hoc way as needed.

What's in the Handbook

- An explanation of prior planning decisions necessary for a successful learning team experience

- Detailed information about each *CASL* chapter and guidance for each meeting

- Resources team members can use to conduct, keep track of, and share their learning and its impact on their students' progress

- *Learning Team Facilitator Handbook DVD: Program and Chapter Introductions* (which we'll call the *Handbook* DVD), designed to introduce the content of the CASL program to others and to provide an advance organizer to the reading of each chapter of the book

Assumptions

We assume that, since you have arrived here and are reading this handbook, you already have made a commitment to improving classroom assessment practice. We assume that your commitment includes providing colleagues (teachers and school leaders) with the time to complete structured learning team experiences in order to become better assessors in the classroom. If this describes you, read on.

If you need to learn more about the CASL program before making such a commitment, we recommend that, before you proceed through the handbook, you watch the DVD presentation, *New Mission, New Beliefs: Assessment* for *Learning*, and read the articles "Assessment for Learning: A Key to Motivation and Achievement" (Stiggins, 2006) and "Inside the Black Box: Raising Standards Through Classroom Assessment" (Black & Wiliam, 1998). You may obtain the DVD free from our website (http://www.ets.org/ati). Also, watch Part 1 of the *Handbook* DVD to understand the central ideas our program is built on.

How to Use This Handbook

This handbook is intended primarily for the team leader or facilitator to use, both before and during the learning team process. Although the *CASL* text is set up so that you can learn without a leader or outside teacher, we recommend that someone—either from within the learning team or a person external to the group—take primary planning responsibility. You may plan as a group or appoint one or more people to take on the job. We encourage anyone involved in planning to read through this handbook in its entirety.

The *Learning Team Facilitator Handbook* is organized into five tabs. Tabs 1, 2, 3, and 5 contain information useful to the learning team leader or facilitator. Tab 4 contains information for all learning team members.

1 *Tab 1 provides the big picture of the goals and content of the* CASL *book, describes the content of the* Handbook DVD *and how to use it, and explains the learning team concept.*

2 *Tab 2 explains a series of decisions to make and actions to take before starting learning teams. It also offers tips for successful learning team experiences and suggested actions administrators can take to support learning teams.*

3 *Tab 3 offers resources for planning each assignment and conducting each meeting.*

4 *Tab 4 includes the resources team members will need to assess, track, and share their own learning and its results.*

5 *Tab 5 describes additional resources available to complement the* CASL *text.*

Goals of the CASL Program

The Classroom Assessment for Student Learning (CASL) program teaches how to do two things: (1) assess accurately; and (2) use assessment to increase motivation and learning. We have developed five keys to quality classroom assessment that will ensure that both happen. These five keys are illustrated in Figure 1.1.

Figure 1.1 **Keys to Quality Classroom Assessment**

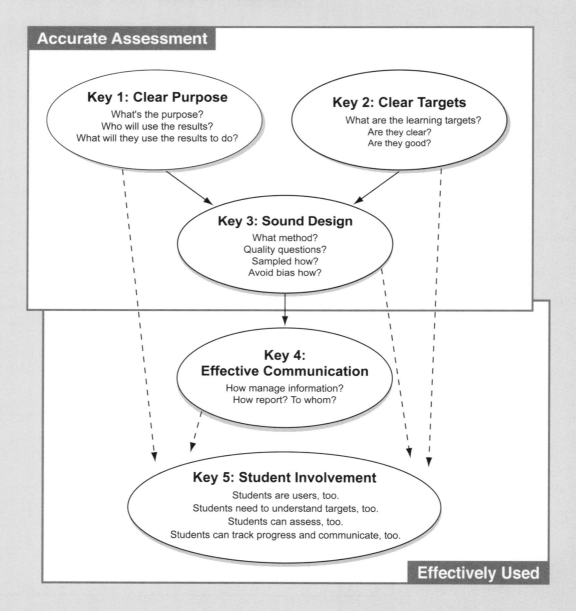

The five keys to quality classroom assessment also define the CASL program goals. Figure 1.2 lays out the practices you will learn or refine through your work with the *CASL* text.

Figure 1.2   **Indicators of Sound Classroom Assesment Practice**

1 Clear Purposes	
Assessment processes and results serve clear and appropriate purposes.	• Teachers understand who the users and uses of classroom assessment information are and know their information needs.
	• Teachers understand the relationship between assessment and student motivation and craft assessment experiences to maximize motivation.
	• Teachers use classroom assessment processes and results formatively (assessment *for* learning).
	• Teachers use classroom assessment results summatively (assessment *of* learning) to inform someone beyond the classroom about students' achievement as of a particular point in time.
	• Teachers have a comprehensive plan over time for integrating assessment *for* and *of* learning in the classroom.

2 Clear Targets	
Assessment reflects clear and valued student learning targets.	• Teachers have clear learning targets for students; they know how to turn broad statements of content standards into classroom-level targets.
	• Teachers understand the various types of learning targets they hold for students.
	• Teachers select learning targets focused on the most important things students need to know and be able to do.
	• Teachers have a comprehensive plan over time for assessing learning targets.

Figure 1.2   (continued)

3 Sound Design Learning targets are translated into assessments that yield accurate results.	• Teachers understand what the various assessment methods are. • Teachers choose assessment methods that match intended learning targets. • Teachers design assessments that serve intended purposes. • Teachers sample learning appropriately in their assessments. • Teachers write assessment questions of all types well. • Teachers avoid sources of mismeasurement that bias results.
4 Effective Communication Assessment results are managed well and communicated effectively.	• Teachers record assessment information accurately, keep it confidential, and appropriately combine and summarize it for reporting (including grades). Such summary accurately reflects current level of student learning. • Teachers select the best reporting option (grades, narratives, portfolios, conferences) for each context (learning targets and intended users). • Teachers interpret and use standardized test results correctly. • Teachers effectively communicate assessment results to students. • Teachers effectively communicate assessment results to a variety of audiences outside the classroom, including parents, colleagues, and other stakeholders.
5 Student Involvement Students are involved in their own assessment.	• Teachers make learning targets clear to students. • Teachers involve students in assessing, tracking, and setting goals for their own learning. • Teachers involve students in communicating about their own learning.

Source: Adapted from Classroom Assessment *for* Student Learning: Doing It Right—Using It Well *(p. 27), by R. Stiggins, J. Arter., J. Chappuis, & S. Chappuis, 2004, Portland, OR: Assessment Training Institute. Copyright 2006, 2004 by Educational Testing Service. Adapted by permission.*

Learning Team Facilitator Handbook DVD: Program and Chapter Introductions

The *Handbook* DVD has two parts:

Part 1   Introduction to the CASL Program

Part 2   Introduction to *CASL* Text Chapters

You can use Part 1 to introduce CASL concepts to others.

Tab 3 provides further information about when to use the Handbook *DVD in learning team meetings.*

Part 1 introduces you to the main concepts of the CASL program. It includes three short segments (10 to 11 minutes each) with Rick Stiggins explaining balanced assessment systems, keys to classroom assessment quality, and the connection between assessment and student motivation. You may want to use one or more of these video clips to help people understand what the CASL program teaches and how classroom assessment can be used to benefit students. The last segment in Part 1 offers a five-minute description of the learning team process and the benefits of this approach to professional development.

Part 2 introduces the reading of each chapter in the *CASL* text. It is designed for facilitators to use with people who have chosen to study classroom assessment using CASL materials, and who have already formed into learning teams. The text of each of the 13 DVD segments is what we would say to introduce each chapter's reading assignment if we were facilitating your learning team meetings. Each segment includes suggestions for materials to have on hand while doing the reading, if needed, and recommendations to carry out selected activities from the chapter.

Features of the *CASL* Text

We include chapter summaries here so that you can get a quick glimpse at the specific lessons taught in *CASL*. It's helpful to refer to the *CASL* Table of Contents as you read through these summaries.

Figure 1.3 **Features of the *CASL* Text at a Glance**

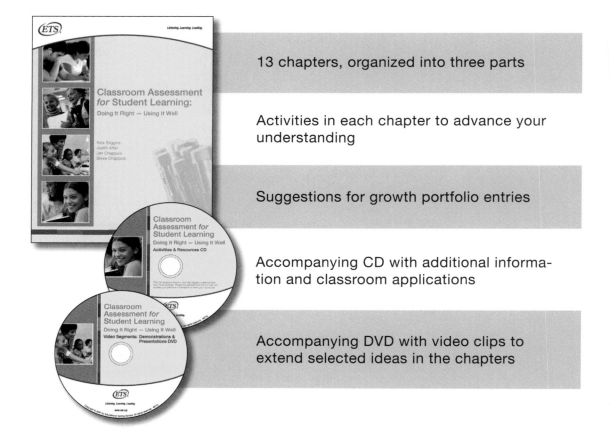

13 chapters, organized into three parts

Activities in each chapter to advance your understanding

Suggestions for growth portfolio entries

Accompanying CD with additional information and classroom applications

Accompanying DVD with video clips to extend selected ideas in the chapters

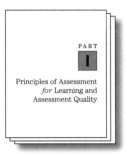

PART
I
Principles of Assessment
for Learning and
Assessment Quality

Part 1 of CASL comprises three chapters and introduces basic concepts that are built on in all of the remaining chapters.

Part 1: Principles of Assessment *for* Learning and Assessment Quality.

Chapter 1, "Classroom Assessment: Every Student a Winner!," gives an overview of the five keys to classroom assessment quality and introduces the learning team approach to using the book.

Chapter 2, "Assessment *for* and *of* Learning," differentiates between the two purposes for assessment, explains the impact of assessment *for* learning on student achievement, establishes the link between assessment and student motivation, and describes seven strategies that encompass assessment *for* learning practices in the classroom.

Chapter 3, "Assess What? Clear Targets," explains the benefits of beginning with clear targets and the kinds of learning targets you are likely to find in your curriculum documents. It offers suggestions for what to do if your learning targets are not clear enough and also shares a procedure for communicating learning targets to students in terms they can understand.

CHAPTER		FOCUS
1	"Classroom Assessment: Every Student a Winner!"	Overview of five keys to assessment quality Introduction to learning team approach
2	"Assessment *for* and *of* Learning"	Differences between assessment *for* and *of* learning Assessment *for* learning's impact on achievement Link between assessment and motivation Seven strategies of assessment *for* learning
3	"Assess What? Clear Targets"	Benefits of clear targets Kinds of learning targets What to do when targets are unclear How to make targets clear to students

The five chapters in Part 2 address issues of accuracy and effective use for each of four assessment methods.

Part 2: Assessment Methods.

Chapter 4, "Assess How? Designing Assessments to Do What *You* Want," describes each of the four assessment methods and shows how to determine when to use which one. It explains each step of the assessment development cycle and offers suggestions for how to use an assessment plan in assessment *for* learning and other student-involvement activities.

Chapter 5, "Selected Response Assessment," begins with a reminder of when this method is most appropriately used. It details the steps involved in developing selected response tests, presents guidelines for evaluating quality, and explains when to use which selected response format. It closes with suggestions for using selected response tests and items as assessments *for* learning.

Chapter 6, "Extended Written Response Assessment," opens with a reminder of when this method is most appropriately used. It explains the steps involved in developing extended written response items and scoring guides, and concludes with ideas for using this method as assessment *for* learning.

Chapter 7, "Performance Assessment," first defines this method and its two parts, tasks and criteria. Next it reviews when performance assessment is most appropriately used and lays out the steps involved in developing a performance assessment. The heart of the chapter focuses on characteristics of high-quality rubrics and tasks. It closes with an extensive list of strategies for using a rubric in assessment *for* learning contexts.

Chapter 8, "Personal Communication as Assessment," begins with a description of conditions to keep in mind before deciding to use this method of assessment. It then outlines types of personal communication assessment formats and offers keys to successful use of each, focusing on personal communication's potential for deepening reasoning proficiencies.

CHAPTER	FOCUS
4 "Assess How? Designing Assessments to Do What *You* Want"	Four assessment methods and when to use each Steps of assessment development cycle Assessment plans as assessment *for* learning
5 "Selected Response Assessment"	How to develop selected response tests Guidelines for quality Selected response formats and when to use each Assessment *for* learning applications
6 "Extended Written Response Assessment"	How to develop extended written response items and scoring guides Scoring options Assessment *for* learning applications
7 "Performance Assessment"	How to critique rubrics and tasks for quality How to develop rubrics and tasks Assessment *for* learning applications
8 "Personal Communication as Assessment"	Conditions to consider before using this method Personal communication assessment options and keys to successful use of each How to use this method to strengthen reasoning proficiencies

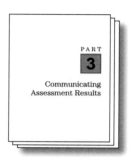

Part 3 focuses on the different ways to communicate about student learning and how to ensure that communication is accurate and effective.

Part 3: Communicating Assessment Results.

Chapter 9, "Communicating About Student Learning," begins with a discussion of the student as primary audience for assessment information. It lays out a plan for balancing assessments *for* and *of* learning in the classroom, explains how to keep track of both kinds of information, and concludes with a discussion of conditions for effective communication.

Chapter 10, "Assessment *of* Learning: Report Cards," opens with a discussion of the purposes for grading and recommendations for which factors to include in the grade. It explains seven grading guidelines, offers six steps to implement these guidelines, and includes a rubric to evaluate classroom grading practices.

Chapter 11, "Portfolios," explores the kinds of portfolios commonly used today, makes recommendations about what to include in a portfolio, and discusses options for judging quality. It concludes with keys to successful use.

Chapter 12, "Conferences About and with Students," describes the purposes for conferences, different formats to accomplish those purposes, and how to conduct meaningful and successful conferences to meet the information needs of students, teachers, and parents.

Chapter 13, "Practical Help with Standardized Tests," emphasizes what educators need to know to use standardized tests most productively to communicate about student achievement and to support learning.

CHAPTER		FOCUS
9	"Communicating About Student Learning"	Balancing assessments *for* and *of* learning Keeping track of information from assessments *for* learning and *of* learning Conditions for effective communication
10	"Assessment *of* Learning: Report Cards"	Purposes for report card grades Factors to include in the grade Grading guidelines Steps in report card grading
11	"Portfolios"	Kinds of portfolios and contents of each Judging quality Options for sharing Keys to success
12	"Conferences About and with Students"	Types of conferences How to prepare for, conduct, and follow up with each type
13	"Practical Help with Standardized Tests"	Common misconceptions Explanation of how standardized tests are created and what different test scores mean Ethical test preparation practices What parents and students need to know

Activities to Advance Your Understanding

We have included three types of activities throughout the chapters to help you learn the material at a faster rate and retain it longer. We encourage you to take the time to complete the activities so that what you are reading will translate into enhanced classroom practice and greater student learning. Figure 1.4 explains the types of activities you will encounter.

Figure 1.4 **Types of Activities in the *CASL* Text**

Type of Activity	In Other Words	Actions	Purpose
"Deepen Understanding"	*"I get it."*	Reflect on a given situation. Create a product.	Enhance your understanding of the concepts presented.
"Try This"	*"I can use it."*	Translate concepts into classroom applications.	Offer hands-on practice.
"Reflect on Your Learning"	*"I know what I know."*	Think about the impact of what you are learning.	Make the information your own.

Suggestions for Growth Portfolio Entries

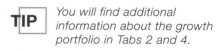

TIP *You will find additional information about the growth portfolio in Tabs 2 and 4.*

At the end of each chapter is a section called "Tracking Your Learning—Possible Portfolio Entries." We encourage learning team members to track their progress and that of their students for three reasons: doing so (1) deepens their commitment to the learning; (2) helps them learn more; and (3) provides a source of intrinsic reward. Plus, with these activities we model assessment *for* learning tactics that we advocate for students.

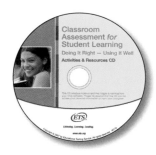

CD Accompanying the *CASL* Book

We have prepared a CD of resources to use while reading the *CASL* text and trying out ideas suggested in the activities. The CD is located in the plastic sleeve in the back of the *CASL* book. Read through Appendix A in *CASL* to get a sense of what kinds of resources are on the *CASL* CD.

DVD Accompanying the *CASL* Book

We have filmed 10 short video segments to elaborate on specific points of the text. They are found on the DVD in the plastic sleeve in the back of the *CASL* book. (Some chapters have one or more DVD clips and some chapters have none.) There is also a related "Deepen Understanding" activity for each clip in its corresponding chapter. Appendix B in *CASL* lists the titles of the video segments and this handbook's Tab 3 includes a brief description of each. Review those descriptions when you're planning learning team meetings, in case you'd like to show and discuss a DVD clip as a team. Otherwise, we recommend that people watch the clips as a part of their individual study of the chapter.

Our Model for Professional Development in Classroom Assessment Competencies*

Depending on how staff development is currently conducted in your school or district, you may need to explain the learning team model: why it is a good idea, what the time commitment will be, why participants are expected to do work between meetings, why you can't just buy good assessments or "workshop" your way through the content, and so forth. You may find the information that follows to be helpful in addressing these and other questions about learning teams, if they arise.

Effective Professional Development

A major staff development challenge all school districts face is providing the right conditions so that teachers can translate new information into effective classroom practice. Our learning team approach to developing classroom assessment expertise is based on best practice as reflected in professional development literature and research: adults learn best when the experience is collaborative, provides active learning opportunities right in the classroom, and focuses on student learning (Figure 1.5). In addition, the positive impact of structured reflection for both students and adults is well documented; few activities are more powerful for professional learning than is reflection on personal practice. Our learning team approach allows participants time to work individually, to try out new ideas in the classroom, and to reflect on their learning with colleagues in small groups.

---

* Portions of this explanation are adapted from Stiggins & Chappuis (2006), pp. 13–14.

Figure 1.5   **Effective Professional Development . . .**

Focuses on improving student learning by enabling teachers to reflect on and improve their classroom practice in specific ways that lead to higher student achievement.

Promotes ongoing, continuous increments of improvement over time.

Relies on the investigation of sound new perspectives and strategies, collaborative interaction, study of the research, and hands-on practice as adult learning tactics.

Is flexible, accommodating differences in teachers' knowledge bases as well as rate of learning.

Is supported with sufficient resources and is economical—it provides maximum impact for resources invested.

The Learning Team Approach

Key Question
A guiding question for learning teams is, "What is happening **differently** in our classrooms *as a result of what we are doing and learning in our teams?"* (Murphy & Lick, 2001, p. 12; emphasis in original).

A learning team is composed of three to six individuals who have committed to meet regularly for an agreed amount of time guided by a common purpose: to help all members increase classroom assessment competence through collaboration during team meetings and individual study and practice between meetings.

Learning team participants engage in a combination of independent study and ongoing small-group collaboration with a commitment to helping all group members develop classroom assessment expertise (Figure 1.6). The process begins with an infusion of new ideas, which can come from several sources: attending workshops, reading books and articles, watching videos, and observing other teachers at work. It continues with ongoing opportunities to discuss and work through changes in

Learning Team Defined
A group of three to six individuals who have committed to independ–ent study and application of ideas, followed by regular meetings to reflect on and improve their assessment practices

The Learning Team's Goal
To help all members refine their assessment practices through collaboration during team meetings and individual study between team meetings

thinking about assessment. But most importantly, it requires that each team member transform new assessment ideas into changes in classroom practices. In this way, they and their students learn valuable lessons about what works for them and why.

When such hands-on learning experiences are shared among teammates in regular team meetings, all members benefit from the lessons of each participant. When teams commit to shaping the ideas into new classroom practice, reflecting on the results, and sharing the benefits with each other, professional growth bears fruit: teams reach their ultimate goal of changing classroom assessment practices in specific ways that benefit students.

Figure 1.6   **The Learning Team Process**

Reading and reflecting on new ideas
Shaping the ideas into classroom applications
Experimenting, observing, drawing inferences about what does and does not work
Summarizing learning and conclusions to share with the learning team
Meeting to discuss and share ideas and practices
Meeting to learn more about selected topics

Why a Learning Team Approach Is Successful

All CASL program materials have been developed for use in learning teams—a professional development model that combines independent and collaborative learning. A learning team approach to professional development succeeds in part because it is job-embedded; its context is the classroom, and it relies on teachers regularly using what they have learned both individually and collaboratively. It is flexible in structure, content, and time; it can be customized to the specific needs of the individual participants and accommodate differences in knowledge base as well as in rate of learning. It is ongoing, and provides the support necessary to initiate and sustain change. It does not rely on the availability of outside experts; rather, it develops internal expertise. Finally, it is a cost-effective use of staff development resources (Figure 1.7).

Figure 1.7   **Benefits of a Learning Team Approach**

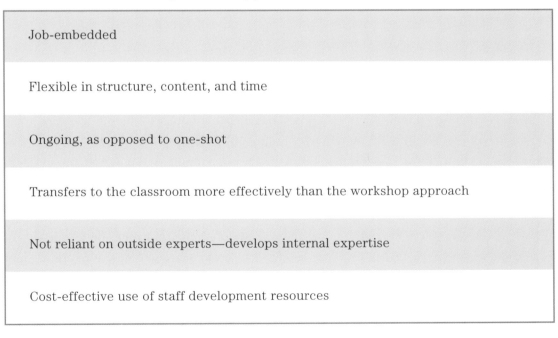

Job-embedded

Flexible in structure, content, and time

Ongoing, as opposed to one-shot

Transfers to the classroom more effectively than the workshop approach

Not reliant on outside experts—develops internal expertise

Cost-effective use of staff development resources

Why Purchasing Assessments Can't Substitute for Professional Development

Off-the-shelf assessments don't help teachers understand or apply the strategies that have been proven to increase student learning. They do not show teachers how to make learning targets clear to students or how to help students understand the differences between strong and weak work. They don't help teachers understand what kinds of feedback are most effective or how to find the time to provide that feedback. Purchased assessments do not help teachers show students how to assess their own strengths and weaknesses, nor do they emphasize the motivational power of having students track and share their learning. They don't guarantee assessment accuracy, and they can't substitute for the professional development needed to cause changes in assessment practice in the classroom.

Why Workshops Alone Won't Suffice

We can't "workshop" our way to assessment competence. A professional development model designed to provide a quick workshop fix or to economize on time at the expense of deep understanding will fail when the content to be delivered is classroom assessment expertise. This is not an initiative. Developing classroom assessment expertise goes beyond teaching people how to create a test or how to convert rubric scores to grades. It requires examining well-established assessment practices that are in fact harmful to students and their learning. It involves learning how to build assessment *for* learning environments that meet both students' and teachers' information needs. It requires teachers to decide what to give up and what to retool. The workshop model of professional development cannot offer the ongoing opportunities for trial, reflection, and support needed for such changes.

Introducing the Concept of Learning Teams to Others

You may want to offer a short presentation to help participants understand learning teams as a professional development option, in which case, consider using one or both of the following two activities. Use the first activity if your audience is not familiar with the concept of collaborative learning or of learning teams as a professional development model. Use the second activity to explain the learning team's goal and process—the details of how learning teams work.

Activity 1: Discussion of Effective Professional Development

In this activity, people read and discuss quotations that represent current thought about effective professional development.

1. Copy the eight quotations in Figure 1.8 (pp. 26–28) so that each person gets one quote. For example, if you have 24 audience members, make 3 copies of the figure and cut the quotes apart so that each person gets one.)

2. Pass out the quotes randomly.

3. Have participants find a partner with a different quote and read their quotes out loud to each other.

4. Partners discuss the extent to which this piece of research or information about effective staff development matches current practice. Or, you may have them discuss the extent to which it matches how they think adults learn most effectively.

5. After about five minutes, participants find another partner with a different quote and repeat the process.

6. Bring participants together as a group to reflect on features of effective professional development. Introduce learning teams as a professional development model that is built on these features.

Activity 2: Presentation to Share Information

We include a default handout (Figure 1.9, pp. 29–30) for this presentation. Please feel free to use it or modify it to suit your context.

Prior to giving this presentation, please read the article, "What a Difference a Word Makes" (Stiggins & Chappuis, 2006), available through a link on our website (**http://www. ets.org/ati**). Also study carefully the rationale, logistics, and tips for success found in Tabs 1 through 4 in this handbook and in *CASL* Chapter 1, pages 19–22.

1. Begin with a definition of learning teams in the CASL program context, explaining how they differ from book discussion groups, and why learning teams are a powerful professional development option.

2. We like to show the seven-minute DVD, *Passion and Persistence: How to Develop a Professional Learning Community* (available at **http://www. solution-tree.com/public/Media.aspx?node=&parent= &ShowDetail=true&ProductID=DVF008** [phone 800-733-6786]) to reinforce the power of collaborative learning. It is both motivating and entertaining, and people generally feel quite positive about collaborating after viewing it.

3. Following the video, explain the learning team's goal and process.

4. Depending on your context, you may wish to ask people to sign up if they are interested in participating in a learning team. Or, this may be an information-only session.

Figure 1.8 **Handouts for Discussion of Effective Professional Development**

Without the focus on improving student learning, educators often could not connect what happened in one year with the next. In fact, using "the pendulum swings" as an excuse for waiting for the next change—not doing any serious thinking about the current thrust because it would be gone next year—is a direct consequence of unfocused professional development. Anticipating four to seven years for the change process to become culturally significant allows educators to continuously analyze needs using a data-driven process centered on student achievement.

Speck, M., & Knipe, C. (2005). Why can't we get it right? Designing high-quality professional development for standards-based schools. *2nd ed. Thousand Oaks, CA: Corwin, p. 6.*

[H]igh-quality professional development deepens teachers' content knowledge and assessment expertise within that content, is embedded in the day-to-day tasks of teaching, draws on internal and external sources of expertise, engages teachers as leaders of staff development efforts as well as learners, . . . and promotes collaborative interaction and inquiry among teachers.

Sparks, D. (2005). Foreword. In Speck, M., & Knipe, C., Why can't we get it right? Designing high-quality professional development for standards-based schools. *2nd ed. Thousand Oaks, CA: Corwin, p. ix.*

[P]rofessional development is a purposeful and intentional process. It is a consciously designed effort to bring about positive change and improvement. Professional development is not, as some perceive it to be, a set of random, unrelated activities that have no clear direction or intent. True professional development is a deliberate process, guided by a clear vision of purposes and planned goals. These goals form the criteria by which content and materials are selected, processes and procedures developed, and assessments and evaluations prepared.

Guskey, T. (2000). Evaluating professional development. *Thousand Oaks, CA: Corwin, p. 17.*

Figure 1.8   (continued)

If there is anything the research community agrees on, it is this: The right kind of continuous, structured teacher collaboration improves the quality of teaching and pays big, often immediate, dividends in student learning and professional morale in virtually any setting. Our experience with schools across the nation bears this out unequivocally.

DuFour, R., Eaker, R., & DuFour, R. (Eds.). (2005). On common ground: The power of professional learning communities. *Bloomington, IN: National Educational Service, p. xii.*

What everyone appears to want for students—a wide array of learning opportunities that engages students in experiencing, creating, and solving real problems, using their own experiences, and working with others—is for some reason denied to teachers when they are learners. . . . [P]eople learn best through active involvement and through thinking about and becoming articulate about what they have learned. Processes, practices, and policies built on this view of learning are at the heart of a more expanded view of teacher development that encourages teachers to involve themselves as learners—in much the same way as they wish their students would.

Lieberman, A. (1995). Practices that support teacher development. Phi Delta Kappan, 76*(8):* *591–596 (quotes from pp. 591, 592).*

The workshop model introduces new strategies into classrooms, but without additional support, fewer than 10% of teachers persist in using new strategies until they integrate them into their repertoire.

When teachers used the new methods immediately and frequently, formed study teams for sharing, observation, and peer coaching, 88% of teachers used new strategies regularly and effectively.

Lashway, L. (1998). Creating a learning organization. ERIC Digest, 21*(April): n.p. Online:* *http://chiron.valdosta.edu/whuitt/files/lrnorg.html* *Retrieved May 30, 2007.*

Figure 1.8 (continued)

If teachers are to successfully teach all students to high standards, virtually everyone who affects student learning must be learning virtually all the time. . . . It is difficult to overestimate the amount of study, practice, classroom coaching, discussion, small group problem solving, and other forms of follow-up that are necessary to change instruction and improve student learning.

Sparks, D. (2000). Foreword. In Guskey, T., Evaluating professional development. *Thousand Oaks, CA: Corwin, pp. ix–x.*

Shifts in Staff Development Practice

FROM training conducted away from the job as the primary delivery system
TO multiple forms of job-embedded learning.

FROM an orientation toward the transmission of knowledge and skills by experts
TO the study by teachers of the teaching and learning processes.

FROM staff developers who function primarily as trainers
TO those who provide consultation, planning, and facilitation services as well as training.

FROM staff development provided by one or two departments
TO staff development as a critical function and major responsibility performed by all administrators and teacher leaders.

Sparks, D., & Hirsch, S. (1997). A new vision for staff development. *Alexandria, VA: Association for Supervision and Curriculum Development.*

Figure 1.9   **Learning Team Introductory Presentation Handout**

Learning Teams

All CASL materials have been developed for use in learning teams—a professional development model that combines independent and collaborative learning.

What Are CASL Learning Teams?

Groups of 3 to 6 individuals who have committed to independent study and application of ideas, followed by regular meetings to reflect on and refine their assessment practices

Why Learning Teams?

Summary of effective professional development:

- Focuses on improving student learning by enabling teachers to reflect on and improve their classroom practice in specific ways that lead to higher student achievement
- Promotes ongoing, continuous increments of improvement over time
- Relies on the investigation of sound new perspectives and strategies, collaborative interaction, study of the research, and hands-on practice as adult learning tactics
- Is flexible, accommodating differences in teachers' knowledge bases as well as rate of learning
- Is supported with sufficient resources and is economical—it provides maximum impact for resources invested

Benefits of a learning team approach to staff development:

- Job-embedded
- Flexible in structure, content, and time
- Ongoing, as opposed to one-shot
- Transfers to the classroom more effectively than the workshop approach
- Not reliant on outside experts—develops internal expertise
- Cost-effective use of staff development resources

Figure 1.9 *(continued)*

The Learning Team's Goal

To help all members refine their assessment practices through collaboration during team meetings and individual study between team meetings

> *What is happening differently* in our classrooms *as a result of what we are doing and learning in our study teams?*
>
> (Murphy & Lick, 2001, p. 12, emphasis in original)

What Is the Learning Team Process?

- Reading and reflecting on new ideas
- Shaping the ideas into classroom applications
- Experimenting, observing, drawing inferences about what does and does not work
- Summarizing learning and conclusions to share with team members
- Meeting to discuss and share ideas and practices
- Meeting to learn more about selected topics

If You Want to Participate in a Learning Team

Who

When

Where

2

Planning for a Successful Learning Team Experience

Purpose	To explain the prior planning decisions necessary for a successful learning team experience
Content	◇ Overview of Tab 2
	◇ Learning team logistics: setup and operation
	◇ Tips for initiating and leading successful learning team experiences
	◇ Roles of building- and district-level administrators

2 Planning for a Successful Learning Team Experience

Overview of Tab 2

Figure 2.5, found on pages 50–52, is a planning form you can copy and use to record your decisions.

In this tab, we lay out a series of planning decisions and provide forms you can use to organize your thinking. Read through Tab 2 before beginning with learning teams. You can do all planning before establishing the team, or you may wish to include the team in making some of the decisions. In the first section, we explain the primary planning considerations summarized in Figure 2.1.

Learning Team Logistics: Setup and Operation

Composition of the Team

Prior to any other decisions, it is necessary to establish whether the learning team experience will be voluntary or mandated. We strongly encourage you to avoid mandating participation. Remember, in this model, team time is to be used as a collaborative learning experience, where people come together to process and build on what they independently have learned and tried. It is very difficult to mandate the reading and application necessary to make this work. If you mandate participation and decide to not require work outside the team meeting time, then the experience becomes a discussion group or a mini-workshop. Both of these options are useful for some learning, but as explained in Tab 1, neither is effective in accomplishing the goal of assessment expertise. We also address the issue in Chapter 1 of *CASL*, pages 19–22.

Figure 2.1   **Planning Considerations**

Composition of the Team

How large will the teams be? How will membership be determined? Will participation be voluntary or mandatory?

Team Leadership

What will the facilitator do?

What form will team leadership take? Will that be decided by the team or established in advance?

Compensation

Will compensation be offered for time beyond the school day? If so, what form(s) will it take?

Scheduling Meetings and Pacing Options

What is the time frame for completion of study? How often will teams meet? How long will each meeting last? Will the team make these decisions or will they be made in advance? By whom?

What reading schedule will the team follow? Will it be set by the team or by someone else?

Team Member Responsibilities

What will the team's responsibilities be? Who will decide?

Work Between Meetings

What work will team members do between meetings? Who will decide?

Meeting Agenda Topics

What will teams do during the meetings? Who will decide?

Learning Team Log

How will teams communicate the work they did during each meeting? To whom?

Tracking and Evaluating Growth

How will team members track their learning? Will they share it? If so, how?

Roles of Building- and District-Level Administrators

Will they participate in leadership learning teams? In learning teams with staff? What other support can they offer?

We recommend a learning team be composed of three to six volunteer members, from the same department or grade level or from a variety of assignments. Learning teams can include administrators and support staff as well as classroom teachers. One of the most important criteria for assembling a team is that all members are free to meet at the same time.

Team Leadership

For an optimal experience, we recommend that someone agrees to serve as facilitator, to act for the good of the team. The main function of the facilitator is to organize and manage the process. We do not encourage the facilitator to take on the role of "expert" in classroom assessment. Remember, the CASL program is structured so that the materials, activities, and expertise that teachers bring to the group all come together to create the learning experience, without direct instruction from a leader. The team's facilitator is the team's manager, not the team's teacher.

Facilitator Responsibilities.

The facilitator can shoulder many or few of the organizational responsibilities, depending on how the team is structured. Teams can be led by one designated leader who performs the additional duties needed for the experience to work, or members may choose to take turns running the meetings. However responsibilities are assigned, one or more people should take on management tasks and complete the following oversight actions:

- Post the schedule of team meetings

- Bring materials needed for the meeting

- Monitor meeting time so all members have the opportunity to share

- Review the next assignment at the end of each meeting

- Complete and post a team meeting log after each meeting

2

In addition, the facilitator helps the team set group operating principles (norms) that foster responsible participation. We have found that teams function best if, as a group, they agree to some version of the following:

- To make team time a priority and to honor the time commitment

- To do the work between meetings, for personal benefit, for the benefit of the students, and for the benefit of the team

- To offer differences of opinion respectfully

- To come prepared to the meetings

- To help each other notice success

Team management responsibilities can be thought of as a continuum that correlates to the degree to which team members are volunteers. In general, if all members of a team have volunteered to participate, outside management consists of helping teams form and providing necessary resources. These teams tend to run independently and to rotate team management responsibilities. Sometimes teams need assistance with understanding or implementing ideas, in which case management consists of obtaining additional resources or expertise. For people who facilitate a number of teams, team management may involve arranging (or presenting) periodic workshops to support the learning. If members are only marginally volunteers or if participation is mandatory, learning team management can require that one person external to the team carefully plan and lead every meeting. Figure 2.2 illustrates this continuum of facilitator involvement.

Figure 2.2   **Learning Team Facilitation—Levels of Involvement**

HIGH INVOLVEMENT

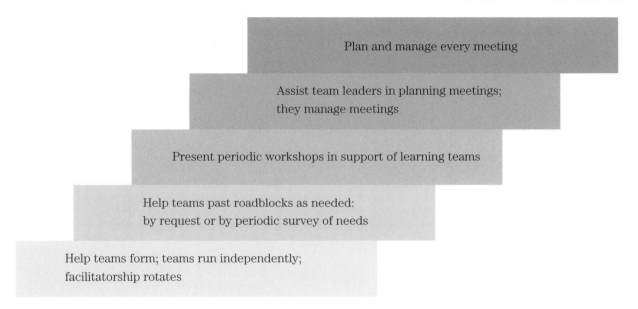

Plan and manage every meeting

Assist team leaders in planning meetings; they manage meetings

Present periodic workshops in support of learning teams

Help teams past roadblocks as needed: by request or by periodic survey of needs

Help teams form; teams run independently; facilitatorship rotates

LOW INVOLVEMENT

Rotating Facilitatorship.

For some groups, especially those whose members have volunteered to participate, the facilitatorship role can rotate. Each member takes a turn at performing agreed facilitator duties, such as those described previously. In this situation, all members take equal responsibility for and have equal ownership in the success of the experience. When participation is involuntary and participants are resistant, this may not be the best choice. Keep in mind, though, that not all involuntary groups are resistant and that rotating facilitatorship may work well to increase ownership of the process.

Designated Facilitator.

Some groups designate one member as the facilitator. It is generally more fruitful if the designated facilitator adopts a learner stance during the meetings and refrains from slipping into the role of "expert" or "presenter." Again, remember that the facilitator is managing the process, not teaching the content. This option can work well whether participation is voluntary or involuntary.

Facilitating Two or More Teams.

If you are facilitating two or more teams, we encourage you to participate with at least one of them. We suggest that teams meeting without you either designate a facilitator or adopt the rotating facilitatorship model. Your role would then be to establish and post a schedule of readings and meetings (or help them do this) and see that they have materials needed for each meeting. You may wish to conduct an initial meeting with the facilitators of each team, or with the teams all together, if facilitatorship will rotate. Figure 2.3 offers a possible agenda for this meeting.

Figure 2.3   **Facilitating More Than One Team**

When you are setting up more than one team, you will want to conduct an initial meeting with the team facilitator(s), or with all team members who will participate, depending on your context. We recommend that you include the following topics in your initial meeting.

Overview

- Goal of the learning teams
- Learning team process
- Our (the participants') commitment

Resources

- Structure of the book
- Structure of the chapters
- *Learning Team Facilitator DVD: Program and Chapter Introductions*
- Other interactive training videos, if used

Between and During Meetings

- What to do at the first meeting
- What to do between meetings (and how to decide, if there are options)
- What to do during meetings (and how to decide, if there are options)
- Establishing group norms
- Meeting dates (number of meetings and dates or date windows for each meeting)
- Meeting length
- Facilitation
- Filling out the learning team log at the end of the meeting

Tracking Growth

- Individual portfolios and possible contents
- Periodic evaluation of classroom assessments
- Student survey
- Other options

Support

- Offer support for learning—let facilitators know they can email you or talk to you with questions, but reinforce that they may have the answers among themselves.
- Plan future events, focused on areas facilitators would like more information about, or on topics their teams would like to explore in more depth.

2

Coordinating a Team Without Participating.

If you are coordinating the team and you are not planning to attend the meetings, we encourage you to establish team leadership as suggested in the previous subsection.

Figure 2.4 summarizes learning team leadership options.

Compensation

Because learning team participation requires at least some work beyond the school day, it is important to acknowledge this and search out compensation options, such as a stipend, an hourly rate (if teams meet outside the work day), credit applied toward advancement on the local salary schedule, or college credit.

Scheduling Meetings and Pacing Options

The time frame for the learning team experience generally spans one or more school years. The time frame may be established at the district level, or by the individual groups.

Schedule one to two hours for each meeting. Learning teams are more effective when all members have time to discuss their thoughts and what they have tried. The amount of time a meeting will take will depend on the number of people in the group and also on how much material you want to focus on during the meeting. If, for example, you have six people, and you plan to address a whole chapter, the meeting will generally take at least 75 minutes. If you don't have that amount of time, form smaller groups or reduce the scope of the meeting's focus. Do both if you have less than an hour per meeting. We recommend that you study no more than one text chapter at a time (with the possible exception of Chapters 1 and 2). Also, many teams have found it advisable to devote more than one meeting to high-interest chapters.

Figure 2.6, found on pages 53–54, is a general explanation of the information you will need to apply for course credit with a college or university.

Figure 2.7, found on pages 55–59, offers suggestions on how to proceed through the CASL text.

Figure 2.4 **Learning Team Leadership Options**

STRUCTURE	DESCRIPTION	CONDITIONS	CAUTION
Rotating facilitatorship	Group decides what facilitator will do and then each member takes a turn being the facilitator	Participation is voluntarily Participants are highly motivated to learn about assessment	May require one person to take initiative if group energy flags
Facilitator designated in advance	Facilitator is assigned to a group Facilitator also functions as a learner with the team	Participation is voluntarily Participants are highly motivated to learn about assessment	Facilitator will do more work than other team members in preparation for meetings
Facilitator designated in advance	Facilitator is assigned to a group Facilitator also functions as a learner with the team	Participation is not completely voluntary Participants are reasonably willing to learn about assessment	Facilitator may feel the need to take on the role of presenter, if all do not do homework Facilitator will do more work than other team members in preparation for meetings
Facilitator designated in advance	Facilitator is assigned to a group Facilitator also functions as a learner with the team	Participation is mandated Some participants are not interested in learning about assessment	Difficult to require between-meeting reading; meetings may become mini-workshops, with participants as passive learners
Facilitator coordinates more than one team	Facilitator leads two or more learning teams Facilitator also functions as a learner with one or more teams	Any of the preceding conditions	Facilitator needs to have extra time available for organizing and attending meetings
Person not a facilitator coordinates more than one team	Coordinator leads a cadre of facilitators and meets with them on an ongoing basis Facilitator does not participate as a learner on a team	Any of the preceding conditions	Coordinator needs to be as familiar with the material to be learned as are the facilitators

Figure 2.8, found on page 60, is an example of the schedule information it is helpful for team members to have.

We recommend that you schedule meetings two to three weeks apart to give people enough time to read and try something out, without having so much time elapse between meetings that members lose track of the thread of their learning. If you need to schedule meetings a month or more apart, you can cover more content, but you will have to allow more time in the meeting for review, discussion, and sharing.

Team Member Responsibilities

Regardless of the kind of leadership the team has and whether participation is voluntary or mandatory, team members' responsibilities are to establish and adhere to group operating principles and to monitor their own adherence. In other words, team members take responsibility for themselves so the facilitator can pay attention to the content of the meeting. In addition (this goes without saying, but we'll say it anyway) all team members commit to completing homework assignments and to attending all meetings.

Work Between Meetings

The forms in this tab have been developed to help you organize the learning team experience. Feel free to use or adapt any that appeal to you and to ignore those that don't work for you.

Participants should plan for two to four hours of independent work time between meetings. Generally, group members individually read and reflect on a chapter (or a portion of a chapter) from *CASL* and view *CASL* DVD segments as suggested in the chapter activities. They also try out one or more of the ideas—activities undertaken with students or actions taken with curriculum or assessments. Groups sometimes agree to try the same thing; other times they try whatever fits their individual contexts at the moment. Separate interactive program videos are available that correlate with several of the chapters; individuals may decide to work through one or more of these videos as suggested in the text as a part of their study of the chapter. Brief descriptions of these videos appear in Tab 3 in the relevant chapters. The descriptions also appear in Tab 5.

Meeting Agenda Topics

We recommend a basic three-part agenda:

1. Discuss the reading

2. Share actions

3. Prepare for the next assignment

Figure 2.9, found on page 61, presents a template you can use to plan each meeting.

Depending on the time and the needs of the team, you may wish to add to or modify this basic format, as described later in this section.

1. *Discuss the Reading.*

Participants may have questions, which the whole group can explore. They may have insights or anecdotes related to the ideas in the text or video. They may have points of disagreement with the content or with each other. If the disagreement is a matter of incomplete understanding of the material, the facilitator can ask questions or offer interpretation. Other disagreements can be noted in the learning team log (see the next subsection), or participants can make a list of issues that arise for them and revisit these periodically throughout the year. Many issues typically resolve themselves as participants move further into the material.

2. *Share Actions.*

Participants share what they tried and their thoughts about how it worked. When the application they selected involves students in some way, the facilitator can ask what effect, if any, they noticed it had on student motivation, attitude, or achievement.

3. *Prepare for the Next Assignment.*

The meeting concludes with planning for the next meeting and a review of the next reading/viewing assignment. If the team is reading a chapter or part of a chapter before the next meeting, the facilitator shares an advance organizer for the content of the chapter, outlining the main points, suggesting activities to

2

complete, and recommending materials to have on hand. As the facilitator, you can either do this yourself, or show the *Handbook* DVD segment for that chapter. (The chapter introductions comprise Part 2 of the DVD.)

Additional Activities.

Depending on time and interest, during the meeting teams may also do one or more of the activities presented in the chapter. Or, teams may decide to devote a meeting to working through an interactive training video, if the chapter has one.

See "Chapter-by-Chapter Information, Agenda Options, and Recommendations for Work Between Meetings" in Tab 3 for suggestions on the structure of each meeting and options for activities.

Learning Team Log

Figure 2.10, found on page 62, shows a sample learning team log.

We recommend that teams keep a log summarizing the content of each meeting. Its main function is to keep others informed about the team's activities and progress. Each meeting's log can be placed in a notebook in the faculty room, distributed to all team members after the meeting, given to the administrator or other person responsible for overseeing learning teams, and/or used as documentation if team members are receiving compensation for their time.

Tracking and Evaluating Growth

TIP *Tab 3 offers more information about how to set up and manage portfolios.*

We encourage participants to establish a portfolio to keep track of, reflect on, and share their learning. Engaging in these processes deepens commitment to the learning, increases the learning, and offers intrinsic reward along the way by developing a sense of accomplishment.

Tips for Initiating and Leading Successful Learning Team Experiences

In our experience with leading learning teams ourselves and with helping others do it too, we have noticed a few "humps" that people typically encounter. We've prepared this list of suggestions to help smooth your path.

1. Understand that developing classroom assessment expertise is not an initiative. It is an essential and powerful component of the job of teaching. Teaching well does not happen *in any context* without it.

2. Give yourself permission to take more than a year to develop assessment expertise. Consider this as a two- to three-year endeavor and pace yourself accordingly. As a district goal, plan for it to take at least five years.

3. Balance your desire to be an expert before leading others with the need to get started. Begin with careful preparation; if this area is not part of your knowledge base, do some advance learning. You can form a small team of colleagues and study the book and videos together, trying the ideas out in your classroom. If you don't have a classroom, borrow one from a teammate and try the ideas or ask to observe while a teammate is trying ideas. But *don't wait too long* before leading others in this study. After gaining a basic understanding of the keys to assessment quality, you can begin to work with others in the role of facilitator or "lead learner." Remember, the CASL program materials are designed so that learning teams can function well without an "expert" on the team.

4. If you are giving an initial presentation to introduce the ideas to others, help your audience understand that the research information and sound assessment practices you will be sharing are *not* theory. Participants are learning what works, why it works, and how to make it work in their classrooms.

5. Be clear about the actions to be taken between meetings. (Sometimes when people are working with Rick DuFour's "Professional Learning Communities" model, they assume that it will lead seamlessly into establishing learning teams. While DuFour's

**Tips for Initiating
and Leading
Successful
Learning Team
Experiences**
(continued)

model does lay a solid foundation for collaborative learning in teams, there is often a difference between the two models in the level of individual responsibility beyond the meeting time.) Look for ways to compensate participants for at least some of this time (e.g., college credit, salary schedule advancement credit, stipend from staff development money or grant money). Also build in periodic opportunities for participants to notice changes in student motivation and achievement that are attributable to changes in assessment practice.

6. If you give a presentation designed to introduce the ideas, contextualize the information: relate lessons, information, and activities to participants' grade levels and subjects taught. Initial examples can be less closely related, but further examples and extended practice should fall within the context of what participants teach and assess on a regular basis.

7. Set group norms that foster responsible participation.

8. Let the structure of the meetings be dictated by the goals of the team and the needs of the team. Don't go overboard on assigning group roles—remember, your team's main focus is a productive assessment learning experience for all members, rather than a cooperative learning exercise. A good set of group norms will serve you well. In the same vein, it is not necessary to teach in-depth group process skills; in an assessment learning team, you will not need to find consensus on difficult issues or make decisions that will adversely affect some members. Disagreements or differences of opinion do not have to be resolved within the context of the team; they need only to be presented respectfully, with the collective goals of the group in mind. The norms your group sets should be sufficient to govern participants' actions.

Roles of Building- and District-Level Administrators*

Sharing Program Goals
The goals of the CASL program, summarized in Tab 1, Figure 1.2, are described in that tab and in CASL, Chapter 1.

Administrative support is crucial to the success of learning teams. The first action building and district instructional leaders can take is to develop an understanding of what the teams are learning. We recommend that you share the central ideas that team learning will focus on with all administrators prior to beginning a learning team study. Rick Stiggins does that in Part 1 of the *Handbook* DVD. You may wish to show this segment to make the ideas clear.

The following suggested actions are designed for building leaders who want to maximize the success of learning teams in their schools.

1. The most effective step you as a principal can take to support learning teams in your school is to join a learning team yourself. More than any other thing you can do, this act telegraphs that you believe assessment literacy to be a high priority, a skill set worthy of your own time. In some cases, building and district administrators form leadership learning teams. These teams can participate in district-level planning using the text *Assessment FOR Learning: An Action Guide for School Leaders*, or they can study the *CASL* text as a group, in preparation for establishing and supporting learning teams at school sites. In other cases, building administrators join staff in their study of *CASL*.

2. As a building principal, hold learning team meeting time sacred. Avoid asking individuals to do something else during their meeting time.

3. Members of the learning teams have committed a great deal of their own time, as well as team time, to develop assessment expertise. They may also be willing to assist you on other committees/teams, but consider not asking them for additional time commitments while this learning team is underway.

---

* *Adapted from Chappuis, Stiggins, Arter, & Chappuis, 2005, pp. 188–189.*

2

4. Learning team members are acting on intrinsic motivation. The greatest reward for them will be seeing the changes in their students. Help them track those changes by asking about them. Encourage members to document students' changes for their own personal growth portfolios. If this seems overwhelming, ask them to select three students—one strong learner, a midrange learner, and a struggling learner—and look for changes in them.

5. If you are a member of a team, consciously adopt a "learner stance." In team or committee settings, some people watch the principal to see how she or he responds and then pattern their actions after the principal's. You want your team members to feel safe enough to admit that something doesn't work well and to try new ideas. Model this thinking: "I always did _____ when I was teaching, and now I see why it wasn't the best choice. If I had it to do over again, I think I'd try _____." In a learning team setting, it can work to your advantage to be a learner along with your staff, and it can work against you if they see you as the "expert;" you have not joined a learning team to teach the class, you are there to participate in collaborative learning.

6. If you are not able to join a team, get a schedule of your teams' meeting dates and assigned readings. Strive at least to be connected to what they are learning. Ask questions about the specific chapters they are reading and what they are doing with those ideas.

7. Identify a "concept of the week" (or month). Highlight it at a staff meeting—through examples, an activity, testimonials, student work, whatever. Consider co-planning the meetings with team facilitators or whole teams.

8. Be quick to notice success. If someone tells you, "I tried this out, and it really worked!" respond to that information. E-mail a question or comment. Recognize small successes; make those small but important changes visible in some way. Get them into faculty meetings—plan a short (5 minute), regular "Successful Assessment Ideas Sharing Time" to help people realize that huge successes build on small ones, and that we/they are learning one step at a time. Celebrate the steps!

9. Ask members of the team to invite you into the classroom the next time they try a new idea. Get in there to watch student involvement in action. "I'm intrigued by . . . and wondered if you would let me know the next time you . . ." Write a short note commenting on one positive aspect of what you saw.

10. Release teachers to watch each other. Substitute for them if need be.

11. Schedule joint planning time for team members to create and/or critique an assessment together.

2

Figure 2.5   **Planning Decisions Form**

Composition of the Team

Will participation be optional?   _____ Voluntary   _____ Mandatory

How many members will be on each team? _____

How will members be assigned to teams? _____

Team Leadership

How will team leadership function?

Facilitator Responsibilities

_____ Rotating facilitatorship   _____ Designated leader   _____ External coordinator

Who will assume the following responsibilities?

_____ Post schedule of meetings

_____ Bring materials needed for the meeting

_____ Review next assignment

_____ Complete and post team meeting log

_____ Monitor meeting time so all members have opportunity to share

_____ Other:_____

Compensation

Will team members be compensated for their work? _____ Yes   _____ No

If so, how?

_____ Stipend

_____ Hourly rate

_____ Local salary schedule credit

_____ College/University credit

_____ Other: _____

Figure 2.5   (continued)

Scheduling Meetings and Pacing Options

Time frame for entire learning team experience: _____

Total number of meetings: _____

Length of each meeting: _____

Amount of time between meetings: _____

Team Member Responsibilities

What will each team member's responsibilities be?

_____ Establish and adhere to group operating principles

_____ Monitor own adherence

_____ Other: _____

Work Between Meetings

Who will determine what work to do between meetings?

_____ Team

_____ Facilitator

_____ Other: _____

Meeting Agenda Topics

Who will decide what the team does during meetings?

_____ Team

_____ Facilitator

_____ Other: _____

Learning Team Log

How will teams keep track of and communicate the work they did during the meetings?

_____ Learning Team Log

_____ Other: _____

Figure 2.5   (continued)

Tracking and Evaluating Growth

Will participants keep a portfolio? _____ Optional   _____ Required

What will they document? _____ Individual decision   _____ Predetermined

What artifacts will they include?

Confidence Questionnaire	_____ Optional	_____ Required
Assessments evaluated for quality	_____ Optional	_____ Required
Student surveys	_____ Optional	_____ Required
Samples of student work	_____ Optional	_____ Required
Other _____	_____ Optional	_____ Required

Roles of Building- and District-Level Administrators

_____ Participate in Leadership Team

   _____ Participate in district planning with *Assessment FOR Learning: An Action Guide for School Leaders*

   _____ Participate in an administrative learning team with *Classroom Assessment* for *Student Learning: Doing It Right—Using It Well*

_____ Participate with staff in a learning team with *Classroom Assessment* for *Student Learning: Doing It Right—Using It Well*

_____ Provide support: _____

_____

_____

_____

Figure 2.6   **Applying for Course Credit**

A person who has adjunct faculty status at a higher education institution can request that the CASL program of study be included in the institution's graduate program offerings. Information needed to establish course credit for the CASL program includes the following:

- The overall course goal
- Specific course objectives
- A description of the mode of study
- The basis for evaluation of learning

Overall Course Goal

You may use a description such as this one to convey the overall course goal:

This professional development program seeks to build a deep and far-reaching understanding of the difference between sound and unsound classroom assessment, promoting the effective use of assessment as a teaching tool. The means selected to reach this goal include having educators study *Classroom Assessment* for *Student Learning: Doing It Right—Using It Well* (2004), by Richard J. Stiggins, Judy Arter, Jan Chappuis, and Steve Chappuis of Educational Testing Service, Portland, Oregon, and its associated print and video training materials.

Specific Course Objectives

To communicate the specific course objectives, you can use the "Indicators of Sound Classroom Assessment Practice," (Figure 1.2 in Tab 1 of this handbook).

Mode of Study

The mode of study can be described as follows:

The primary organizational structure of this program of study is the learning team. Working in groups of three to six, participants will proceed chapter by chapter through the text, relying on assignments described within, supplementary videos, and readings as needed, to strengthen their assessment literacy. The learning teams and leadership within teams will be coordinated at the local district level.

Figure 2.6 (continued)

The amount of work to be completed will require a time investment of 4 to 6 hours per text chapter, including reading, reflecting, completing associated assignments, and team work. Thus, the total work time will average 65 hours. Of this, expect two-thirds to involve individual study, reflection, and application in the classroom, and one-third to involve cooperative efforts within the learning team.

Basis for Evaluation

Each higher education institution offering credit for completion of this program will have its own requirements for evaluation and grading; however, educators participating in this program are completing a number of activities as part of their studies that provide an excellent basis for this evaluation.

1. **Confidence Questionnaire.** Participants are asked to complete a survey at the beginning, middle, and end of study that tracks growing confidence with the topics and major ideas in the materials.

2. **Application Activities.** The text includes various activities designed to enhance, extend, and apply learning. These include case studies, video discussions, worksheet discussions, analysis of existing classroom assessments for quality, construction of assessments, and things to try with students.

3. **Classroom Assessment Professional Growth Portfolio.** Over the term of study, each participant gathers and presents to the team evidence of increasing mastery of assessment literacy. The individual record of improvement takes the form of a portfolio. A detailed description appears in Tab 4 of this handbook.

Some combination of these activities and artifacts can provide the instructor of record with evidence of achievement from which to judge student performance. However, decisions about appropriate standards, criteria, and grading practices are left to the credit-granting institution.

Source: Adapted from Classroom Assessment *for* Student Learning: Doing It Right—Using It Well *(CD-ROM, n.p.), by R. Stiggins, J. Arter., J. Chappuis, & S. Chappuis, 2004, Portland, OR: Assessment Training Institute. Copyright 2006, 2004 by Educational Testing Service. Adapted by permission.*

Figure 2.7 **Pacing Options for the Study of *CASL***

Chapter	Content/Major Activities	Pacing Options
1	**"Classroom Assessment: Every Student a Winner!"** • Understand the big picture of assessment quality: accuracy + effective use • Suggestions for forming a team and learning together • Suggestions for tracking your learning	This chapter is usually the focus of only one meeting. Some teams cover the basics of Chapter 1 in an introductory presentation and combine the reading of Chapters 1 and 2 as the focus for their first learning team meeting. **Related video:** *New Mission, New Beliefs: Assessment* for *Learning*
2	**"Assessment *for* and *of* Learning"** • Understand the differences between assessments *of* and *for* learning, the impact of assessment *for* learning on student motivation and achievement, and the power of descriptive feedback • Establish a preliminary vision of what assessment *for* learning looks like in the classroom • Suggestions for tracking your learning	Some groups spend two or three sessions developing an understanding of assessment *for* learning, doing one or more of Activities 2.1–2.5 as a team. **Related video:** *Assessment* for *Student Motivation*
3	**"Assess What? Clear Targets"** • Understand the role that clear targets play in assessment quality • Define and clarify your own learning targets • Identify which of four kinds of learning targets your own targets are • Create student-friendly versions • Deconstruct standards • Suggestions for tracking your learning	Districts focusing on clarifying content standards or on curriculum mapping may choose to devote two or more sessions to Chapter 3, deepening understanding of their curriculum documents and further clarifying learning targets. They may do one or more of Activities 3.1–3.11 as a team. **Related video:** *Assessing Reasoning in the Classroom*

Figure 2.7   (continued)

Chapter	Content/Major Activities	Pacing Options
4	**"Assess How? Designing Assessments to Do What *You* Want"** • Understand the four assessment methods available • Know when to use which method • Be familiar with the five stages in assessment development • Audit own assessments for match to what is taught • Make test plans for assessments you currently give • Make a test plan for an assessment you want to create, identifying the targets to be assessed and the relative importance of each • Suggestions for tracking your learning	We strongly recommend that you spend two or three sessions on this chapter, engaging in one or more of Activities 4.3–4.7 as a team. Groups that are developing common assessments take additional time with this chapter as they plan their assessments. **Related video:** *Evaluating Assessment Quality: Hands-On Practice*
5	**"Selected Response Assessment"** • Know when to use selected response assessment • Understand how to plan and develop a selected response test • Know when to use which format • Audit test items for adherence to standards of quality • Use selected response tests as assessment *for* learning • Suggestions for tracking your learning	Teachers who create, use, or wish to create or use selected response tests in the classroom may choose to spend two or more sessions on this chapter, doing some or all of Activities 5.3–5.11 as a team. **Related videos:** *Commonsense Paper and Pencil Assessments* *Assessing Reasoning in the Classroom*

Figure 2.7   (continued)

Chapter	Content/Major Activities	Pacing Options
6	**"Extended Written Response Assessment"** • Know what to consider before choosing this method • Understand how to plan and develop an extended written response assessment • Understand options for scoring procedures • Audit extended written response items and scoring guides for quality • Use extended written response assessments as assessment *for* learning • Suggestions for tracking your learning	Teachers who create, use, or wish to create or use extended written response assessments in the classroom may choose to spend two or more sessions on this chapter, doing some or all of Activities 6.3–6.7 as a team. **Related video:** *Assessing Reasoning in the Classroom*
7	**"Performance Assessment"** • Know when to use a performance assessment • Understand how to develop rubrics and tasks • Audit performance tasks and rubrics for quality • Use performance assessments as assessment *for* learning • Suggestions for tracking your learning	Teachers who create, use, or wish to create or use performance assessments in the classroom may choose to spend two or more sessions on this chapter, doing some or all of Activities 7.3–7.11 as a team. **Related video:** *Designing Performance Assessments* for *Learning* **Related book:** *Creating & Recognizing Quality Rubrics*
8	**"Personal Communication as Assessment"** • Know when to use personal communication assessment • Understand the options for types of personal communication assessment • Be aware of possible sources of bias that can distort results • Use personal communication assessment options as assessment *for* learning • Suggestions for tracking your learning	Teachers who rely in large part on personal communication as an assessment method in the classroom may choose to spend two or more sessions on this chapter, doing some or all of Activities 8.3–8.5 as a team.

Figure 2.7 (continued)

Chapter	Content/Major Activities	Pacing Options
9	**"Communicating About Student Learning"** • Know how to balance assessments *for* and *of* learning and how to motivate practice without grading everything • Make appropriate information management decisions • Understand conditions for effective communication • Know how to meet student and parent information needs • Suggestions for tracking your learning	Most teams spend one session on this chapter.
10	**"Assessment *of* Learning: Report Cards"** • Identify the purpose of report card grades • Understand three grading principles • Follow guidelines for accurate grading • Understand steps in report card grading • Evaluate own grading practices • Suggestions for tracking your learning	Many teams spend two or more sessions on this chapter, completing some or all of Activities 10.3–10.10 together. **Related video:** *Grading & Reporting in Standards-Based Schools* **Related book:** *A Repair Kit for Grading: 15 Fixes for Broken Grades*
11	**"Portfolios"** • Know what portfolio options are available and when to use each • Know what to include in a portfolio • Understand options for judging quality • Understand options for sharing portfolio contents • Understand keys to successful use • Analyze your own portfolio	Teams wishing to implement portfolio use spend two or more sessions with this chapter, planning what they will do and what students will do. In addition, they may complete Activities 11.3–11.5 as a team.

Figure 2.7   (continued)

Chapter	Content/Major Activities	Pacing Options
12	**"Conferences About and with Students"** • Be familiar with the variety of purposes for conferences • Know how to select among options • Understand what needs to be in place for each option to be successful • Suggestions for tracking your learning	Teams wishing to implement student-involved conferences spend two or more sessions with this chapter, planning what they will do and what students will do. In addition, they may complete Activities 12.3–12.5 as a team. **Related video:** *Student-Involved Conferences*
13	**"Practical Help with Standardized Tests"** • Understand terms associated with standardized tests • Understand what different test scores mean • Understand effective use and ethical test preparation • Know how to discuss tests and results with parents and students • Suggestions for tracking your learning	Most teams spend one or two sessions with this chapter, clearing up misconceptions and doing one or more of Activities 13.4–13.7 as a group.

Figure 2.8   **Meeting Schedule Planning Form**

Meeting no.	Date	Time	Location	Facilitator	Assignment before Meeting
1					
2					
3					
4					
5					
6					
7					
8					
9					
10					
11					
12					
13					
14					
15					
16					
17					
18					

Source: From Classroom Assessment *for* Student Learning: Doing It Right—Using It Well *(CD-ROM, n.p.), by R. Stiggins, J. Arter., J. Chappuis, & S. Chappuis, 2004, Portland, OR: Assessment Training Institute. Copyright 2006, 2004 by Educational Testing Service. Reprinted by permission.*

Figure 2.9 **Learning Team Meeting Planning Template**

Date: **Start Time:** **End Time:**

1. Discussion of Prior Reading

Chapter/pages read: Time allocated:

Points to address:

2. Discussion of Classroom Applications

Time allocated:

Points to address:

3. Activity/-ies (optional)

Time allocated: Materials needed:

Activity # _____:

Activity # _____:

4. Set up for Next Assignment

Reading:

Activity/-ies to try before next meeting:

Next Meeting Date: **Time:**

Facilitator: **Location:**

Figure 2.10 **Sample Learning Team Log**

Meeting No. _____

Date: _____ Facilitator: _____

Time: _____ to _____ Location: _____

Group Members Present:

Group Member(s) Absent:

Summary of Discussion and Activities:

Classroom applications since last meeting—what we've tried:

For the next meeting we need to do the following:

Next scheduled meeting:

Date: _____ Time: _____

Location: _____ Facilitator: _____

Source: Adapted from Classroom Assessment *for* Student Learning: Doing It Right—Using It Well *(CD-ROM, n.p.), by R. Stiggins, J. Arter., J. Chappuis, & S. Chappuis, 2004, Portland, OR: Assessment Training Institute. Copyright 2006, 2004 by Educational Testing Service. Adapted by permission.*

3

Leading and Managing the Learning Team Experience

Purpose	To give detailed information about each *CASL* chapter and guidance for each meeting
Content	◆ Overview of Tab 3
	◆ Chapter-by-chapter information, resources, agenda options, and recommendations for work between meetings

3 Leading and Managing the Learning Team Experience

Overview of Tab 3

In this tab, we provide the resources you will need to conduct each learning team meeting.

You will want to share a few things with learning team participants before they begin reading the *CASL* text. Tab 3 opens with a description of an introductory meeting agenda detailing the information we recommend you give them. The rest of Tab 3 proceeds chapter by chapter with the following information to help you plan each team meeting:

- A list of the chapter's main points

- A summary of the *CASL* DVD segment or segments that go along with the chapter, if any

- A summary of the related ETS interactive training video that extends the learning of the chapter, if any

- Meeting agenda options for the chapter

- A list of recommended activities to complete before the next meeting

- A handout for team members to use to plan their work between meetings

At the conclusion of this tab, we offer suggestions for a final team meeting. Teams will have formed a bond through the work they have done together; it is a good idea to plan a culminating event, during which they can share and celebrate their achievements. We describe two options, one for sharing within the team and the other for sharing across teams or with a larger audience.

Chapter-by-Chapter Information, Agenda Options, and Recommendations for Work Between Meetings

Chapter Information

The first part of each chapter entry in this tab offers summary information about the chapter and related resources:

- We begin with a summary of the chapter's main ideas for you to refer to as you think about what activities you may want to recommend that team members do, both before and during the chapter's meeting.

- We then summarize the content of any *CASL* DVD clip or clips that accompany the chapter, so that you can decide whether to recommend the team watch the clip either before or during the meeting.

- Last, we describe the content of any interactive training video that complements the ideas in the chapter, again so that you can decide if and when to use it.

Agenda Options

In the second part of each chapter's entry in this tab, we lay out possible agenda options for the meeting that follows the reading of that chapter. These recommendations reflect the most significant ideas and activities in the chapter, and include tips about both what participants might have a hard time understanding and concepts that tend to require more time to process. In the suggestions for previewing the next chapter, we sometimes recommend an activity to do during the meeting that will link the ideas of the two chapters, if you have time. We also direct you to a *Handbook* DVD segment to provide an advance organizer of the next reading.

Recommendations for Work Between Meetings

In the third part, we offer recommendations for what participants can do between meetings. We begin with instructions for you to give to team members as needed. Then we list activities to complete during the reading of the chapter, representing a menu of options. You (or the team as a whole) will want to select from this list by considering what concepts or actions are most important and relevant to the team's learning.

Handout for Participants

Through experience working with hundreds of learning teams over the past 10 years, we have learned that one of the keys to success is organized communication about what individual team members are to do between meetings. Even if team members are deciding for themselves what they will do, it helps to have a way to keep track of specific actions to be taken. So, you will find a form preceding each chapter's entry in this tab that you can give to participants to organize their work before that chapter's meeting.

The handout includes the chapter's main points, a place to note the pages to read, and a complete list of the chapter's activities, set up so that participants can check those they intend to complete. Recommended activities are listed first. You will also find a place on the handout to note the next meeting date, time, location, and materials to bring.

Recommended Activities in Each Chapter

Why are only some of the activities in each chapter recommended?

If you have time, we would suggest that you complete all of the activities that accompany each chapter. However, some are more central to comprehending the text and others function as extensions of learning.

The activities we recommend you complete between meetings are those we consider to be of the highest priority. They have the following characteristics:

1. *They help you process the information or they make it clearer.*

2. *They can be done individually.*

3. *They can be completed no matter what you teach.*

4. *They provide good discussion points at the meeting.*

3

The Introductory Team Meeting

The purpose of the introductory team meeting is to set up the learning. This meeting will have three topics: the "what"—the content of the learning; the "how"—the learning team process; and the "when"—the logistics. At the conclusion of the meeting, you will give the first reading assignment and any activity assignments you may have chosen.

The Content of the Learning

 The article, "What a Difference a Word Makes" (Stiggins & Chappuis, 2006) available through a link on our website (http://www.ets.org/ati) summarizes the first two topics.

You may wish to read it before holding the first meeting.

Six Agenda Items for the Introductory Meeting

1. Overview of the goals of the program—the content of the learning

2. Overview of the learning team process

3. Determining leadership structure, facilitator responsibilities, team members' responsibilities, and group operating principles

4. Determining or sharing the meeting schedule

5. Planning for tracking growth

6. Giving the first assignment

Briefly review the goals of the program (found in Tab 1 and Tab 4). Explain or review how they fit into the mission of the school or district. If you want to have Rick Stiggins explain the five keys to quality to your group, you could show the segment of Part 1 on the *Handbook* DVD titled "Assessment Quality" as an introduction to the content of study.

The Learning Team Process

Share or review a brief description of the learning team model of professional development (found in Tab 1). Make sure participants understand that they will be engaged in reading and trying ideas out between team meetings as a part of this commitment.

Learning Team Logistics

If not determined in advance, one of your first decisions is how to structure team leadership: whether you will have a designated facilitator or will rotate leadership. Then agree on the facilitator's responsibilities. We recommend that whoever does the facilitating completes the following oversight actions:

- Post a schedule of team meetings

- Bring materials needed for the meeting

- Monitor meeting time so all members have the opportunity to share

- Review the next assignment at the end of each meeting

- Complete and post a team meeting log after each meeting

Following this, agree on the responsibilities of team members. We suggest that those include establishing and adhering to group operating principles and monitoring their own adherence. Consider adopting some version of the following operating principles (discussed previously in Tab 2):

Learning Team Agreements

We will

- Do the work—the reading and whatever activities we have selected.

- Stick to the topic or task during the meeting.

- Keep the focus on students.

- Involve everyone. Make sure all voices are heard.

- Be active listeners. Seek to understand as well as to be understood.

Meeting Schedule

Determine your meeting schedule if it has not been determined in advance. Decide when and where to meet and establish a reading and assignment schedule.

Tracking Growth

 Instruments and forms learning team members can use to track their learning appear in Tab 4.

Plan for how each team member will keep track of and evaluate growth. Use a working folder or notebook to collect the work. Options for tracking and evaluating growth include the following:

- "Confidence Questionnaire"

- Reflective journal entries

- Evaluations of assessments used/modified during the course of study

- Student surveys

- "Before," "during," and "after" samples of student work

- Other activities chosen to document specific learning or accomplishments

Setting Up the Reading

Share an advance organizer of the main ideas in Chapter 1. You can use the Chapter 1 segment in Part 2 of the *Handbook* DVD to do this.

Recommended Activities to Complete Before Meeting 1

Facilitator as Participant

If you are participating on the learning team, we suggest that you also do the recommended activities.

Have participants read Chapter 1, pages 3–28, and do one or more of the following:

- Activity 1.2: Emily's Interview, page 7

- Activity 1.3: Case Comparison: Emily and Krissy, page 10

- Activity 1.4: Case Comparison: Emily and Mr. Heim's Class, page 12

- Activity 1.5: Evaluating Assessment Quality, page 19

- Activity 1.7: Classroom Assessment Confidence Questionnaire, page 28

Remind them to consider which artifacts, if any, to place in their professional growth portfolios.

Chapter 1—Classroom Assessment: Every Student a Winner!

Main Points   **Reading Assignment: Pages** _____

- Introduction to five keys to quality assessment
- Introduction to learning teams
- Overview of the program—learning targets and materials

Recommended Activities to Complete (check the ones you plan to do)

- ❑ Activity 1.2: Emily's Interview, p. 7
- ❑ Activity 1.3: Case Comparison: Emily and Krissy, p. 10
- ❑ Activity 1.4: Case Comparison: Emily and Mr. Heim's Class, p. 12
- ❑ Activity 1.5: Evaluating Assessment Quality, p. 19
- ❑ Activity 1.7: Classroom Assessment Confidence Questionnaire, p. 28
- ❑ Select portfolio entries.

Additional Activities You May Wish to Complete

- ❑ Activity 1.1: Program Introduction, p. 4
- ❑ Watch Video, *New Mission, New Beliefs: Assessment* for *Learning*

- ❑ Other: _____

_____

_____

_____

_____

Next Meeting Date: _____   **Time:** _____

Location: _____   **Bring:** _____

Chapter 1

Classroom Assessment: Every Student a Winner!

Main Points

- Introduction to five keys to quality assessment

- Introduction to learning teams

- Overview of the program—learning targets and materials

CASL DVD Segments

"Program Introduction" (10:30)

Rick Stiggins provides a brief overview of the core understandings that gave rise to the ETS professional development program. He outlines the program's goals and highlights several of its key features.

"Learning Teams" (3:30)

Teachers and administrators from Bloomington, Illinois, describe their experience with learning teams as the staff development model they used to become proficient with classroom assessment.

"Interview with Emily" (6:20)

The day after the board meeting described in Chapter 1, Emily discusses her development as a writer in Ms. Weathersby's classroom and her feelings as she told her story to the school board. (Please note that this is a simulated interview.)

Related ETS Video

"New Mission, New Beliefs: Assessment *for* Learning" (50:00)

In this video, Rick Stiggins presents an overview of the history of assessment in school, the changing expectations we have for assessment, and why quality classroom assessment is essential for student success.

You may obtain the DVD New Mission, New Beliefs: Assessment *for* Learning *free from our website (http://www. ets.org/ati).*

Agenda Options for Meeting 1

Discussion of Chapter 1.

- Short, open-ended reaction time to information in text.

- Discuss responses to Activities 1.2–1.4 and how they compared to the five keys to quality.

- Short discussion of which artifacts, if any, from this reading to place in participants' professional portfolios. You may wish to refer them to "Indicators of Sound Classroom Assessment Practice" from Chapter 1, page 27, as a guide for selecting artifacts. That list lays out the program goals, or learning targets, for this course of study.

Preview of Chapter 2.

Share an advance organizer of main ideas in Chapter 2. You can use the Chapter 2 segment in Part 2 of the *Handbook* DVD to do this.

Between Meetings: Recommended Activities to Complete While Reading Chapter 2

 Remind team members to consider which artifacts to place in their professional growth portfolios.

> Have participants read Chapter 2, pages 29–51, and do one or more of the following:
>
> - Activity 2.1: Introduction to Assessment *for* Learning, page 31
>
> - Read through the seven strategies of assessment *for* learning on pages 42–46. Mark those you are familiar with—those you've done or seen done.
>
> - Activity 2.4: Student Survey, page 49
>
> - Activity 2.5: Where Am I Now?, pages 50–51
>
> - Look for an idea from Chapter 2 to try out in the classroom.

Chapter 2—Assessment *of* and *for* Learning

Main Points   **Reading Assignment: Pages** _____

- Explanations of assessment *for* and assessment *of* learning
- Impact of assessment *for* learning
- Assessment and student motivation
- Research on feedback
- What assessment *for* learning looks like in the classroom

Recommended Activities to Complete (check the ones you plan to do)

❑ Activity 2.1: Introduction to Assessment *for* Learning, p. 31

❑ Activity 2.4: Student Survey, p. 49

❑ Activity 2.5: Where Am I Now?, pp. 50 and 51

❑ Look for an idea from Chapter 2 to try out in the classroom.

❑ Select portfolio entries.

Additional Activities You May Wish to Complete

❑ Activity 1.6: Watch Video, *Assessment* for *Student Motivation*, p. 19

❑ Activity 2.2: Assessment, Achievement, and Motivation, p. 41

❑ Read through the seven strategies of assessment *for* learning on pp. 42–46. Mark those you are familiar with—those you've done or seen done.

❑ Activity 2.3: Critique an Assessment for Clear Purpose, p. 47

❑ Other: _____

_____

_____

_____

_____

Next Meeting Date: _____   **Time:** _____

Location: _____   **Bring:** _____

Chapter 2

Assessment *for* and *of* Learning

Main Points

- Explanations of assessment *for* and assessment *of* learning

- Impact of assessment *for* learning

- Assessment and student motivation

- Research on feedback

- What assessment *for* learning looks like in the classroom

CASL DVD Segments

"Assessment OF/FOR Learning" (10:15)

Rick Stiggins compares the purposes of assessment *of* learning (to check achievement status) and assessment *for* learning (to improve achievement), describing what they have in common and what is unique to each.

"Impact of Student-Involved Assessment" (8:00)

Several teachers describe what happened to their teaching and their students' learning when they wove assessment *for* learning strategies into their instruction. Several students also share their perspectives.

Related ETS Interactive Training Video

Assessment *for* Student Motivation (45:00)

In this video, Rick Stiggins explains why the behavior management model of rewards and punishments has not been a productive way to think about assessment. He then offers a new vision, explaining the relationships among student-involved assessment *for* learning, student confidence, and student achievement.

Agenda Options for Meeting 2

Discussion of Chapter 2 Reading and Activities.

- Short, open-ended reaction time to information in text.

- Discuss the balance between assessment *of* learning events and assessment *for* learning events in the classroom. What percentage of assessments that students encounter fall into each category?

- Discuss which of the seven strategies participants are familiar with. Help them notice that the strategies are not necessarily new—the importance here is that they are defined and organized so they can be used intentionally.

- Did participants try anything out in the classroom based on the Chapter 2 reading? Sharing of experiences.

- Short discussion of which artifacts, if any, from this reading to place in participants' professional portfolios. You may wish to refer them to "Indicators of Sound Classroom Assessment Practice" from Chapter 1, page 27, as a guide for selecting artifacts.

Preview of Chapter 3.

You can link Chapters 2 and 3 together by doing Activity 3.1, "Turning Learning Targets into Student-Friendly Language," page 59, if you have time. Point out that this activity is an application of Strategy 1 of the seven strategies. Brainstorm classroom uses of student-friendly language. Or, you can suggest it as homework or do it as an activity at the next meeting.

Share an advance organizer of the main ideas in Chapter 3. You can use the Chapter 3 segment in Part 2 of the *Handbook* DVD to do this.

3

Between Meetings: Recommended Activities to Complete While Reading Chapter 3

Remind team members to consider which artifacts to place in their professional growth portfolios.

Suggest that participants get a copy of their district, state, or provincial curriculum to refer to as they read Chapter 3. Have them read Chapter 3, pages 53–86, and do one or more of the following:

- Activity 3.1: Turning Learning Targets into Student-Friendly Statements, page 59. Do this with a learning target you are currently teaching and share it with students. Summarize the results of doing this to share with the team.

- Activity 3.2: Identifying Knowledge Targets, page 62

- Activity 3.3: Identifying Reasoning Verbs, page 65

- Activity 3.5: Identifying Reasoning Targets, page 69

- Activity 3.7: Identifying Skill Targets, page 72

- Activity 3.8: Identifying Product Targets, page 73

- Activity 3.10: Deconstructing Standards, page 83

Chapter 3—Assess What? Clear Targets

Main Points   **Reading Assignment: Pages** _____

- Benefits of beginning with clear targets
- Kinds of targets: knowledge, reasoning, skill, and product
- Learning targets, state standards, and curriculum
- Deconstructing standards and turning targets into student-friendly language

Recommended Activities to Complete (check the ones you plan to do)

- ❑ Activity 3.1: Turning Learning Targets into Student-Friendly Language, p. 59. Do this with a learning target you are currently teaching and share it with students. Summarize the results of doing this to share with the team.
- ❑ Activity 3.2: Identifying Knowledge Targets, p. 62
- ❑ Activity 3.3: Identifying Reasoning Verbs, p. 65
- ❑ Activity 3.5: Identifying Reasoning Targets, p. 69
- ❑ Activity 3.7: Identifying Skill Targets, p. 72
- ❑ Activity 3.8: Identifying Product Targets, p. 73
- ❑ Activity 3.10: Deconstructing Standards, p. 83
- ❑ Select portfolio entries.

Additional Activities You May Wish to Complete

- ❑ Activity 3:4: Identifying Inductive and Deductive Reasoning, p. 66
- ❑ Activity 3.6: Watch Video, *Assessing Reasoning in the Classroom*, p. 72
- ❑ Activity 3.9: Curriculum Discussion, p. 80
- ❑ Activity 3.11: Critique an Assessment for Clear Targets, p. 85

- ❑ Other: _____

_____

_____

_____

_____

Next Meeting Date: _____   **Time:** _____

Location: _____   **Bring:** _____

Chapter 3

Assess What?
Clear Targets

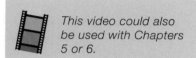

This video could also be used with Chapters 5 or 6.

3

Main Points

- Benefits of beginning with clear targets

- Kinds of targets: knowledge, reasoning, skill, and product

- Learning targets, state standards, and curriculum

- Deconstructing standards and turning targets into student-friendly language

Related ETS Interactive Training Video

Assessing Reasoning in the Classroom (68:00)

Rick Stiggins offers practical, effective ways to use assessments to teach reasoning and to help students succeed at problem solving.

Agenda Options for Meeting 3

Discussion of Chapter 3 Reading and Activities.

- Short, open-ended reaction time to information in text.

- Discuss responses to the activities where participants found examples of the kinds of learning targets in their curriculum documents. Pay close attention to targets they identify as performance skill and product targets. You may want the group to reread the definitions of those two kinds of targets and carefully examine their own selections.

- Participants share learning targets in student-friendly language they created and the effect, if any, of sharing them with students.

- Discussion of other things participants did with the content of Chapter 3.

- Short discussion of which artifacts, if any, from this reading to place in participants' professional portfolios. You may wish to refer them to "Indicators of Sound Classroom Assessment Practice" from Chapter 1, page 27, as a guide for selecting artifacts.

Preview of Chapter 4.

You can link Chapters 3 and 4 by doing Activity 4.4, "Analyze Your Own Assessment for Clear Targets," pages 108–109, using a simple test from your own context, if you have time. Or, you can suggest it as homework or do it together at the next meeting.

Share an advance organizer of the main ideas in Chapter 4. You can use the Chapter 4 segment in Part 2 of the *Handbook* DVD to do this.

Between Meetings: Recommended Activities to Complete while Reading Chapter 4

Remind team members to consider which artifacts to place in their professional growth portfolios.

Have participants read Chapter 4, pages 89–121, and do one or more of the following:

- Activity 4.2: Target–Method Match, pages 96–98. Print out the Chapter 4 CD file, "Target–Method Match Chart," to keep track of your responses.

- Activity 4.4: Analyze Your Own Assessment for Clear Targets, pages 108–109, using an assessment you currently give. Print out the Chapter 4 CD file, "Analyze for Clear Targets," to use in creating your test plan.

- Activity 4.6: Critique an Assessment for Good Design, pages 120–121

Chapter 4—Assess How? Designing Assessments to Do What *You* Want

Main Points   **Reading Assignment: Pages** _____

- Assessment methods: selected response, extended written response, performance assessment, personal communication
- Target–method match
- Assessment development cycle
- Assessment *for* learning applications

Recommended Activities to Complete (check the ones you plan to do)

❑ Activity 4.2: Target–Method Match, pp. 96–98. Print out the Chapter 4 CD file, "Target–Method Match Chart," to keep track of your responses.

❑ Activity 4.4: Analyze Your Own Assessment for Clear Targets, pp. 108–109, using an assessment you currently give. Print out the Chapter 4 CD file, "Analyze for Clear Targets," to use in creating your test plan.

❑ Activity 4.6: Critique an Assessment for Good Design, pp. 120–121

❑ Select portfolio entries.

Additional Activities You May Wish to Complete

❑ Activity 4.1: Which Method?, p. 95

❑ Activity 4.3: Analyze Samples for Target–Method Match, p. 106

❑ Activity 4.5: Video Discussion of *Evaluating Assessment Quality*, p. 119

❑ Activity 4.7: Critique Your Own Assessment, p. 121

❑ Other: _____

_____

_____

_____

_____

Next Meeting Date: _____   **Time:** _____

Location: _____   **Bring:** _____

Chapter 4

Assess How? Designing Assessments to Do What *You* Want

This video could also be used with Chapters 5 or 6.

Main Points

- Assessment methods: selected response, extended written response, performance assessment, personal communication

- Target–method match

- Assessment development cycle

- Assessment *for* learning applications

Related ETS Interactive Training Video

Evaluating Assessment Quality: Hands-On Practice (36:00)

> The video begins with Rick Stiggins and Judy Arter teaching the standards of assessment quality. Viewers are then given the opportunity to critique assessments against the standards.

Agenda Options for Meeting 4

Discussion of Chapter 4 Reading and Activities.

- Short, open-ended reaction time to information in text.

- Discuss responses to "Target–Method Match" activity—any surprises or confusion?

- Discuss results of analyzing their own assessments for clear targets.

- Be prepared to support the need for creating a test plan in advance of teaching the material. You might do this by asking your team to discuss the following open-ended statement: "Without knowing what each item on a test measures, we can't . . ."

- Use the *CASL* CD-ROM file, "Assessment Quality Rubrics," to evaluate an assessment for the trait of Sound Design. You may either do the activity with an assessment from the team or with any one of those in the CD Chapter 3 file, "Assessments to Evaluate."

3

- View segments of the video, *Evaluating Assessment Quality: Hands-On Practice*, to give more practice in evaluating assessments for keys to quality.

- Short discussion of which artifacts, if any, from this reading to place in participants' professional portfolios. You may wish to refer them to "Indicators of Sound Classroom Assessment Practice" from Chapter 1, page 27, as a guide for selecting artifacts.

Preview of Chapter 5.

You can link Chapters 4 and 5 together by doing Activity 5.7, "Engaging Students in Self-Reflection and Goal Setting with Selected Response Tests," page 158, if you have time. Or, you can suggest it as homework or do it as an activity at the next meeting.

Share an advance organizer of the main ideas in Chapter 5. You can use the Chapter 5 segment in Part 2 of the *Handbook* DVD to do this.

Between Meetings: Recommended Activities to Complete While Reading Chapter 5

Remind team members to consider which artifacts to place in their professional growth portfolios.

Refer to CASL pages 273–275 for further suggestions.

Have participants read Chapter 5, pages 123–166, and do one or more of the following:

- Activity 5.2: Create a Quiz, page 127

- Activity 5.3: Make a Test Plan for Your Quiz, page 133

- Activity 5.4: Writing Propositions for Your Quiz, page 135

- Activity 5.6: Critique the Items in Your Quiz, page 151

- Activity 5.7: Engaging Students in Self-Reflection and Goal Setting with Selected Response Tests, page 158

- Activity 5.9: Critique a Selected Response Test You Use, page 165

- Try one assessment *for* learning activity from pages 152–163 with students. Summarize the results to share with the team.

Chapter 5—Selected Response Assessment

Main Points

Reading Assignment: Pages _____

- When to use selected response tests
- Steps in developing selected response tests
- Guidelines for quality
- When to use which format
- Using selected response tests as assessment *for* learning

Recommended Activities to Complete (check the ones you plan to do)

❑ Activity 5.2: Create a Quiz, p. 127

❑ Activity 5.3: Make a Test Plan for Your Quiz, p. 133

❑ Activity 5.4: Writing Propositions for Your Quiz, p. 135

❑ Activity 5.6: Critique the Items in Your Quiz, p. 151

❑ Activity 5.7: Engaging Students in Self-Reflection and Goal Setting with Selected Response Tests, p. 158

❑ Activity 5.9: Critique a Selected Response Test You Use, p. 165

❑ Try one assessment for learning activity from pp. 152–163 with students. Summarize the results to share with the team.

❑ Select portfolio entries.

Additional Activities You May Wish to Complete

❑ Activity 5.1: Learning Targets Best Assessed with Selected Response, p. 126

❑ Activity 5.5: Franzipanics, p. 139

❑ Activity 5.8: Create a Selected Response Test, p. 164

❑ Activity 5.10: Critique "Fish Tank," page165

❑ Activity 5.11: Watch Video, *Commonsense Paper and Pencil Assessments*, p. 165

❑ Other: _____

_____

_____

_____

_____

Next Meeting Date: _____   **Time:** _____

Location: _____   **Bring:** _____

Chapter 5

Selected Response Assessment

Main Points

- When to use selected response tests

- Steps in developing selected response tests

- Guidelines for quality

- When to use which format

- Using selected response tests as assessment *for* learning

Related ETS Interactive Training Video

Commonsense Paper and Pencil Assessments (56:00)
Rick Stiggins shows how to design paper and pencil tests and shares strategies for using them to increase student motivation and achievement.

Agenda Options for Meeting 5

Discussion of Chapter 5 Reading and Activities.
- Discuss issues or questions around the planning and development stages, if needed. Understanding the information about writing propositions may require a little extra team process time.

- Note that there are more examples of reasoning item formulas (pages 146 and 147) in the Chapter 5 CD file, "Reasoning Item Formulas."

- Team members discuss what assessment *for* learning activities they tried and what effect they had on their teaching or on the students' learning.

- Discussion of other things participants did with the content of Chapter 5.

- Short discussion of which artifacts, if any, from this reading to place in participants' professional portfolios. You may wish to refer them to "Indicators of Sound Classroom Assessment Practice" from Chapter 1, page 27, as a guide for selecting artifacts.

- Optional:

  1. Do Activity 5.5, "Franzipanics," page 139, to review main points of item quality.

  2. Critique "Fish Tank" (Chapter 5 CD file, "Assessments to Evaluate") using the checklist on pages 150–151 to review main points of item quality.

  3. View videos: *Commonsense Paper and Pencil Assessments* and/or *Assessing Reasoning in the Classroom.*

Preview of Chapter 6.

Share an advance organizer of the main ideas in Chapter 6. You can use the Chapter 6 segment in Part 2 of the *Handbook* DVD to do this.

Between Meetings: Recommended Activities to Complete While Reading Chapter 6

Remind team members to consider which artifacts to place in their professional growth portfolios.

Refer to CASL pages 273–275 for further suggestions.

Have participants read Chapter 6, pages 167–187, and do one or more of the following:

- Activity 6.1: Learning Targets Best Assessed with Extended Written Response, page 170

- Activity 6.2: Create an Extended Written Response Assessment, page 174

- Activity 6.3: Revise Your Exercise, page 177

- Activity 6.4: Check your Scoring Criteria, page 180

- Activity 6.6: Analyze Your Own Extended Written Response Assessments for Quality, page 187

- Try one assessment *for* learning activity from pages 185–186 with students. Summarize the results to share with the team.

Chapter 6—Extended Written Response Assessment

Main Points   **Reading Assignment: Pages** _____

- When to use extended written response assessment
- Steps in developing extended written response assessments
- Scoring options
- Using extended written response assessments as assessment *for* learning

Recommended Activities to Complete (check the ones you plan to do)

❏ Activity 6.1: Learning Targets Best Assessed with Extended Written Response, p. 170

❏ Activity 6.2: Create an Extended Written Response Assessment, p. 174

❏ Activity 6.3: Revise Your Exercise, p. 177

❏ Activity 6.4: Check your Scoring Criteria, p. 180

❏ Activity 6.6: Analyze Your Own Extended Written Response Assessments for Quality, p. 187

❏ Try one assessment for learning activity from pp. 185–186 with students. Summarize the results to share with the team.

❏ Select portfolio entries.

Additional Activities You May Wish to Complete

❏ Activity 6.5: Analyze Extended Written Response Assessments, p. 182

❏ Activity 6.7: Develop an Extended Written Response Assessment, p. 187

❏ Other: _____

_____

_____

_____

_____

Next Meeting Date: _____   **Time:** _____

Location: _____   **Bring:** _____

Chapter 6

Extended Written Response Assessment

Main Points

- When to use extended written response assessment

- Steps in developing extended written response assessments

- Scoring options

- Using extended written response assessments as assessment *for* learning

Agenda Options for Meeting 6

Discussion of Chapter 6 Reading and Activities.

- Discuss issues or questions around writing the exercise and preparing a scoring mechanism. Participants may want to share their revised exercises and scoring procedures.

- Do Activity 6.5, "Analyze Extended Written Response Assessments for Quality," pages 182–185.

- Team members discuss what assessment *for* learning activities they tried and what effect they had on their teaching or on the students' learning.

- Short discussion of which artifacts, if any, from this reading to place in participants' professional portfolios. You may wish to refer them to "Indicators of Sound Classroom Assessment Practice" from Chapter 1, page 27, as a guide for selecting artifacts.

Preview of Chapter 7.

Share an advance organizer of the main ideas in Chapter 7. You can use the Chapter 7 segment in Part 2 of the *Handbook* DVD to do this.

3

Remind team members to consider which artifacts to place in their professional growth portfolios.

Refer to CASL pages 273–275 for further suggestions.

Between Meetings: Recommended Activities to Complete While Reading Chapter 7

Suggest that participants collect one or two rubrics/scoring guides and one or two performance assessment tasks/assignments they currently use to refer to as they read this chapter. Have them read Chapter 7, pages 189–249, and do one or more of the following:

- Activity 7.1: Learning Targets Best Assessed with Performance Assessment, page 197

- Activity 7.4: Analyze Your Own Rubrics, page 218. Print out the Chapter 7 CD file, "Metarubric," to use. Revise your own rubric, if needed, based on your observations.

- Activity 7.6: Critique Performance Tasks, page 230. Print out the Chapter 7 CD file, "Performance Task Rubric," to use. Revise your own task, if needed.

- Activity 7.8: Student-Friendly Rubric Language, page 233

- Activity 7.9: Adapt Strategies 1 and 2, page 236. Try Strategies 1 and 2 (pp. 232–236) in your classroom with a rubric you know to be of high quality. Summarize the results to share with your team.

- Practice giving descriptive feedback using one of the procedures outlined in Chapter 7, pages 236–239.

Chapter 7—Performance Assessment

Main Points

- What performance assessment is
- When to use performance assessment
- Steps in developing performance assessments
- Developing rubrics and tasks
- Critiquing rubrics and tasks
- Using rubrics as instructional tools in the classroom

Recommended Activities to Complete (check the ones you plan to do)

❑ Activity 7.1: Learning Targets Best Assessed with Performance Assessment, p. 197

❑ Activity 7.4: Analyze Your Own Rubrics, p. 218. Print out the Chapter 7 CD file, "Metarubric," to use. Revise your own rubric, if needed, based on your observations.

❑ Activity 7.6: Critique Performance Tasks, p. 230. Print out the Chapter 7 CD file, "Performance Task Rubric," to use. Revise your own task, if needed.

❑ Activity 7.8: Student-Friendly Rubric Language, p. 233

❑ Activity 7.9: Adapt Strategies 1 and 2, p. 236. Try Strategies 1 and 2 (pp. 232–236) in your classroom with a rubric you know to be of high quality. Summarize the results to share with your team.

❑ Practice giving descriptive feedback using one of the procedures outlined in Chapter 7, pp. 236–239.

❑ Select portfolio entries.

Additional Activities You May Wish to Complete

❑ Activity 7.2: Determining Sample Size, p. 199

❑ Activity 7.3: Develop a Rubric, p. 217

❑ Activity 7.5: Develop a Performance Task, p. 225

❑ Activity 7.7: Watch DVD Segment, "Teachers on Rubrics," p. 232

❑ Activity 7.10: Create a Student-Involved Performance Assessment Plan, p. 243

❑ Activity 7.11: Watch Video, *Designing Performance Assessments* for *Learning*, p. 243

❑ Activity 7.12: Term Paper Assignment, p. 246

❑ Activity 7.13: Help Students Understand Performance Criteria, p. 246

❑ Other: _____

_____

Next Meeting Date: _____   **Time:** _____

Location: _____   **Bring:** _____

3

Chapter 7

Performance Assessment

Main Points

- What performance assessment is

- When to use performance assessment

- Steps in developing performance assessments

    1. Developing rubrics and tasks

    2. Critiquing rubrics and tasks

- Using rubrics as instructional tools in the classroom

CASL DVD Segment

"Teachers on Rubrics" (7:30)

Teachers from different grade levels and school subjects detail both how they have used student-involved performance assessment in their classrooms and what effects it has had on student achievement.

Related ETS Interactive Training Video

Designing Performance Assessments *for* Learning (75:00)

Judy Arter and Jan Chappuis show how to evaluate rubrics and performance tasks for quality. This video also includes a segment on how to develop a rubric, with examples taken from the work of a team of science teachers.

Agenda Options for Meeting 7

Discussion of Chapter 7 Reading and Activities.

- Discuss what participants discovered when they went through the chapter with their own rubrics and tasks.

- Participants share what they did with Strategies 1 and 2 and effects, if any, they noticed on students' motivation or learning. They also share any other activities they tried with students.

- Discuss the results of the descriptive feedback assignment—the effects on student motivation and learning.

- Short discussion of which artifacts, if any, from this reading to place in participants' professional portfolios. You may wish to refer them to "Indicators of Sound Classroom Assessment Practice" from Chapter 1, page 27, as a guide for selecting artifacts.

- Optional: Watch all or portions of the video, *Designing Performance Assessments* for *Learning*. It presents an updated explanation of task quality, rubric quality, and how to develop a rubric from scratch. It also includes a streamlined rubric for rubrics and rubric for tasks, which are easier to use than the ones accompanying Chapter 7. Those rubrics can also be found in *Creating & Recognizing Quality Rubrics* (Arter & Chappuis, 2006).

Preview of Chapter 8.

Share an advance organizer of the main ideas in Chapter 8. You can use the Chapter 8 segment in Part 2 of the *Handbook* DVD to do this.

Between Meetings: Recommended Activities to Complete While Reading Chapter 8

Remind team members to consider which artifacts to place in their professional growth portfolios.

Refer to CASL pages 273–275 for further suggestions.

Have participants read Chapter 8, pages 251–275, and do one or more of the following:

- Activity 8.1: Learning Targets Best Assessed with Personal Communication, page 254

- Activity 8.2: Generate Oral Questions, page 260

- Try one assessment *for* learning activity. Summarize the results to share with your team. If you use journals with students, consider using Activity 8.5: Journal Icons, page 269.

In addition, Activity 8.3: Practice Questioning Strategies, page 260, can be done as a coaching activity between meetings.

Chapter 8—Personal Communication as Assessment

Main Points   **Reading Assignment: Pages** _____

- When to use personal communication as assessment
- Types of personal communication assessment: instructional questions and answers, conferences and interviews, class discussions, oral examinations, journals and logs
- Possible sources of bias that can distort results

Recommended Activities to Complete (check the ones you plan to do)

❑ Activity 8.1: Learning Targets Best Assessed with Personal Communication, p. 254

❑ Activity 8.2: Generate Oral Questions, p. 260

❑ Try one assessment *for* learning activity. Summarize the results to share with the team.

❑ Select portfolio entries.

Additional Activities You May Wish to Complete

❑ Activity 8.3: Practice Questioning Strategies, p. 260

❑ Activity 8.4: Scored Discussion, p. 263

❑ Activity 8.5: Journal Icons, p. 269

❑ Other: _____

_____

_____

_____

_____

Next Meeting Date: _____   **Time:** _____

Location: _____   **Bring:** _____

Chapter 8

Personal Communication as Assessment

Main Points

- When to use personal communication as assessment

- Types of personal communication assessment: instructional questions and answers, conferences and interviews, class discussions, oral examinations, journals and logs

- Possible sources of bias that can distort results

CASL DVD Segment

"Personal Communication" (10:20)

Tia Wulff, an elementary teacher, describes using instructional questions with her students as a source of insight into their learning. She also offers her thoughts on using personal communication effectively as an assessment method.

Agenda Options for Meeting 8

Discussion of Chapter 8 Reading and Activities.

- Short, open-ended reaction time to information in text.

- Discuss conclusions and observations from homework activities.

- Team members discuss what assessment *for* learning activities they tried and what effect they had on their teaching or on the students' learning.

- Discussion of other things participants did with the content of Chapter 8.

- Short discussion of which artifacts, if any, from this reading to place in participants' professional portfolios. You may wish to refer them to "Indicators of Sound Classroom Assessment Practice" from Chapter 1, page 27, as a guide for selecting artifacts.

3

Preview of Chapter 9.

You can introduce Chapter 9 by doing Activity 9.1, "Synergy Between Assessments *for* and *of* Learning in Your Classroom," page 284, if you have time. Or, you can suggest it as homework or do it as an activity at the next meeting.

Share an advance organizer of the main ideas in Chapter 9. You can use the Chapter 9 segment in Part 2 of the *Handbook* DVD to do this.

Between Meetings: Recommended Activities to Complete While Reading Chapter 9

 Remind team members to consider which artifacts to place in their professional growth portfolios.

Refer to CASL pages 273–275 for further suggestions.

Suggest that participants have their gradebooks handy to refer to as they read. Have them read Chapter 9, pages 279–299, and do one or more of the following:

- Activity 9.1: Synergy Between Assessments *for* and *of* Learning in Your Classroom, page 284

- Activity 9.2: Auditing for Balance, page 285

- Watch the Chapter 9 DVD segment, "Record Keeping" (referred to on page 291).

- Activity 9.4: Revisit Grading Key—4, 3, 2, 1, X, page 297

Chapter 9—Communicating About Student Learning

Main Points

Reading Assignment: Pages _____

- Balancing assessments *for* and *of* learning
- Tracking information from assessments *for* and *of* learning
- Conditions for effective communication
- Meeting student and parent needs

Recommended Activities to Complete (check the ones you plan to do)

❑ Activity 9.1: Synergy Between Assessments *for* and *of* Learning in Your Classroom, p. 284

❑ Activity 9.2: Auditing for Balance, p. 285

❑ Watch the Chapter 9 DVD segment, "Record Keeping" (referred to on p. 291).

❑ Activity 9.4: Revisit Grading Key—4, 3, 2, 1, X, p. 297

❑ Select portfolio entries.

Additional Activities You May Wish to Complete

❑ Activity 9.3: Managing Achievement Information for Emily's Classroom, p. 291

❑ Activity 9.5: Critique an Assessment for Good Communication, p. 299

❑ Other: _____

_____

_____

_____

_____

Next Meeting Date: _____   **Time:** _____

Location: _____   **Bring:** _____

3

Chapter 9

Communicating About Student Learning

3

Main Points

- Balancing assessments *for* and *of* learning

- Tracking information from assessments *for* and *of* learning

- Conditions for effective communication

- Meeting student and parent needs

CASL DVD Segment

"Record Keeping" (6:00)

Jan Chappuis draws on the distinction between assessment *for* and *of* learning to lay out the information management challenges present. She shares a commonsense approach to tracking each kind of information.

Agenda Options for Meeting 9

Discussion of Chapter 9 Reading and Activities.

- Short, open-ended reaction time to information in text.

- Team members discuss similarities and differences between their gradebooks and examples in the text.

- Short discussion of which artifacts, if any, from this reading to place in participants' professional portfolios. You may wish to refer them to "Indicators of Sound Classroom Assessment Practice" from Chapter 1, page 27, as a guide for selecting artifacts.

Preview of Chapter 10.

Share an advance organizer of the main ideas in Chapter 10. You can use the Chapter 10 segment in Part 2 of the *Handbook* DVD to do this.

Between Meetings: Recommended Activities to Complete While Reading Chapter 10

Remind team members to consider which artifacts to place in their professional growth portfolios.

Suggest that participants have their gradebooks and any grading procedures that exist in writing (e.g., their own formulae for determining grades, the district's percent-to-grade conversion scale) handy to refer to as they read. Have them read Chapter 10, pages 301–333, and do one or more of the following:

- Activity 10.2: What Are Your Purposes for Grades?, page 305

- Activity 10.4: Agatha's Writing Grade, page 317

- Activity 10.5: Assigning a Final Grade, page 322

- Activity 10.6: Your Own Grading Process, page 326

- Activity 10.8: Analyzing Your Own Grading Practices, page 332

3

Chapter 10—Assessment *of* Learning: Report Cards

Main Points

- The purpose of report card grades
- Factors to include in the grade
- Grading principles and guidelines
- Steps in the report card grading process
- Rubric for grading practices

Reading Assignment: Pages _____

Recommended Activities to Complete (check the ones you plan to do)

- ❏ Activity 10.2: What Are Your Purposes for Grades?, p. 305
- ❏ Activity 10.4: Agatha's Writing Grade, p. 317
- ❏ Activity 10.5: Assigning a Final Grade, p. 322
- ❏ Activity 10.6: Your Own Grading Process, p. 326
- ❏ Activity 10.8: Analyzing Your Own Grading Practices, p. 332
- ❏ Select portfolio entries.

Additional Activities You May Wish to Complete

- ❏ Activity 10.1: Reflect on Current Practice, p. 303
- ❏ Activity 10.3: The Dilemma of Late Work, p. 307
- ❏ Activity 10.7: Watch Video, *Grading & Reporting in Standards-Based Schools*, p. 327
- ❏ Activity 10.9: Your Friend's Gradebook, p. 332
- ❏ Activity 10.10: Converting Your Own Rating Scales to Grades, p. 333

- ❏ Other: _____

_____

_____

_____

_____

Next Meeting Date: _____   **Time:** _____

Location: _____   **Bring:** _____

Chapter 10

Assessment *of* Learning: Report Cards

Main Points

- The purpose of report card grades

- Factors to include in the grade

- Grading principles and guidelines

- Steps in the report card grading process

- Rubric for grading practices

Related ETS Interactive Training Video

Grading & Reporting in Standards-Based Schools (60:00)

> Rick Stiggins and Ken O'Connor guide viewers through a discussion of the most compelling issues related to collecting evidence of student achievement and lay out a process to develop more effective grading practices.

Agenda Options for Meeting 10

Discussion of Chapter 10 Reading and Activities.

- Short, open-ended reaction time to information in text.

- Discuss conclusions participants drew from homework activities.

- Discuss what participants decided about their own grading practices. (This can be a lengthy and lively discussion.)

- Discuss what changes, if any, participants are considering making with their grading practices. (This also has potential for a lively discussion.)

- Optional: Watch the video, *Grading & Reporting in Standards-Based Schools*, to review the components to be included in a grade and important considerations in creating a defensible grading scheme.

3

3

- Short discussion of which artifacts, if any, from this reading to place in participants' professional portfolios. You may wish to refer them to "Indicators of Sound Classroom Assessment Practice" from Chapter 1, page 27, as a guide for selecting artifacts.

Preview of Chapter 11.

Share an advance organizer of the main ideas in Chapter 11. You can use the Chapter 11 segment in Part 2 of the *Handbook* DVD to do this.

Between Meetings: Recommended Activities to Complete While Reading Chapter 11

 Remind team members to consider which artifacts to place in their professional growth portfolios.

Have participants read Chapter 11, pages 335–355, and do one or more of the following:

- Activity 11.1: Job Interview Simulation, page 339

- Activity 11.2: What Type of Portfolio Is This?, pages 351–352

- Activity 11.4: Analyze Your Own Growth Portfolio, page 358

- Activity 11.5: Plan for Students, page 359

- Try one idea from Chapter 11 with students. Summarize your and their reactions to the experience.

As participants read through Chapter 11, they will probably have some thoughts about their own portfolios. Suggest that they take a few moments at the conclusion of the chapter to examine what they have collected so far and to make any adjustments that may have come to mind during the reading.

Chapter 11—Portfolios

Main Points   **Reading Assignment: Pages** _____

- Kinds of portfolios: project, growth, achievement, competence, celebration, working folders
- Portfolio contents: artifacts, work sample annotations, goal setting, student self-reflection
- Judging quality
- Options for sharing
- Keys to successful use

Recommended Activities to Complete (check the ones you plan to do)

❑ Activity 11.1: Job Interview Simulation, p. 339

❑ Activity 11.2: What Type of Portfolio Is This?, pp. 351–352

❑ Activity 11.4: Analyze Your Own Growth Portfolio, p. 358

❑ Activity 11.5: Plan for Students, p. 359

❑ Try one idea from Chapter 11 with students. Summarize your and their reactions to the experience.

❑ Select portfolio entries.

Additional Activities You May Wish to Complete

❑ Activity 11.3: The Dilemma of Student Selection and Clear Communication, p. 356

❑ Other: _____

_____

_____

_____

_____

Next Meeting Date: _____   **Time:** _____

Location: _____   **Bring:** _____

Chapter 11

Portfolios

Main Points

- Kinds of portfolios: project, growth, achievement, competence, celebration, working folders

- Portfolio contents: artifacts, work sample annotations, goal setting, student self-reflection

- Judging quality

- Options for sharing

- Keys to successful use

Agenda Options for Meeting 11

Discussion of Chapter 11 Reading and Activities.

- Short, open-ended reaction time to information in text.

- Discuss conclusions participants drew from homework activities.

- Participants share what action they took, if any, as a result of reading Chapter 11, and what effect it had on their teaching or on students' learning.

- Short discussion of which artifacts, if any, from this reading to place in participants' professional portfolios. You may wish to refer them to "Indicators of Sound Classroom Assessment Practice" from Chapter 1, page 27, as a guide for selecting artifacts.

Preview of Chapter 12.

Share an advance organizer of the main ideas in Chapter 12. You can use the Chapter 12 segment in Part 2 of the *Handbook* DVD to do this.

Between Meetings: Recommended Activities to Complete While Reading Chapter 12

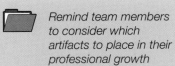

Remind team members to consider which artifacts to place in their professional growth portfolios.

Have participants read Chapter 12, pages 361–386, and do one or more of the following:

- Activity 12.1: Your Experiences with Conferences, page 363

- Activity 12.2: Set a Goal for Learning, page 374. Print out the Chapter 12 CD file, "Goal-Setting Frames," for use here.

- Activity 12.3: Comparing Conference Experiences to Ideas in the Chapter, page 383

- Try one idea from Chapter 12 with students. Summarize your and their reactions to the experience.

3

Chapter 12—Conferences About and with Students

Main Points   **Reading Assignment: Pages** _____

- Types of conferences: feedback, goal-setting, intervention, demonstration of growth, and achievement conferences
- How to prepare for, conduct, and follow up with each type

Recommended Activities to Complete (check the ones you plan to do)

❑ Activity 12.1: Your Experiences with Conferences, p. 363

❑ Activity 12.2: Set a Goal for Learning, p. 374. Print out the Chapter 12 CD file, "Goal-Setting Frames," for use here.

❑ Activity 12.3: Comparing Conference Experiences to Ideas in the Chapter, p. 383

❑ Try one idea from Chapter 12 with students. Summarize your and their reactions to the experience.

❑ Select portfolio entries.

Additional Activities You May Wish to Complete

❑ Activity 12.4: Watch Video, *Student-Involved Conferences*, p. 383

❑ Activity 12.5: The High School Faculty Debate on Student-Led Conferences, p. 385

❑ Other: _____

_____

_____

_____

_____

Next Meeting Date: _____   **Time:** _____

Location: _____   **Bring:** _____

Chapter 12

Conferences About and with Students

Main Points

- Types of conferences: feedback, goal-setting, intervention, demonstration of growth, and achievement conferences

- How to prepare for, conduct, and follow up with each type

CASL DVD Segment

"Student-Involved Portfolio Conferences" (17:20)

Tia Wulff enumerates a variety of practical keys to success in conducting student-involved conferences, sharing her perspective on their effects on student confidence, motivation, and learning.

Related ETS Interactive Training Video

Student-Involved Conferences (60:00)

Anne Davies and Rick Stiggins share effective ways to prepare students to participate in conferences and keys to productive student-involved conferences. Viewers have the option of participating in a simulation of a student-led conference to translate the information into practice.

Agenda Options for Meeting 12

Discussion of Chapter 12 Reading and Activities.

- Short, open-ended reaction time to information in text.

- Discuss what participants tried with students in the classroom. What were their reactions? What was the effect on motivation? On learning?

- Short discussion of which artifacts, if any, from this reading to place in participants' professional portfolios. You may wish to refer them to "Indicators of Sound Classroom Assessment Practice" from Chapter 1, page 27, as a guide for selecting artifacts.

Preview of Chapter 13.

Share an advance organizer of the main ideas in Chapter 13. You can use the Chapter 13 segment in Part 2 of the *Handbook* DVD to do this.

Between Meetings: Recommended Activities to Complete While Reading Chapter 13

 Remind team members to consider which artifacts to place in their professional growth portfolios.

Have participants read Chapter 13, pages 387–429, and do one or more of the following:

- Activity 13.1: Standardized Tests Used in Your District, pages 389–390

- Activity 13.2: A Definitions Pretest, page 390

- Activity 13.3: Hills' Handy Hints, page 399

- Activity 13.4: Interpret Your Own Standardized Test Report, page 409

- Activity 13.5: Use Item Formulas to Help Students Learn, page 412

- Activity 13.6: Translate Standardized Test Jargon into Student-Friendly Language, page 414

- Activity 13.7: When Grades Don't Match the State Assessment Results, page 427

- Activity 13.8: A Definitions Posttest, page 428

- Try one idea from Chapter 13 with students. Summarize your and their reactions to the experience.

- Plan for sharing your portfolio.

Chapter 13—Practical Help with Standardized Tests

Main Points   **Reading Assignment: Pages** _____

- Important definitions and common misconceptions
- How standardized tests are developed; what test scores mean
- Measurement error
- Using standardized tests to promote learning
- Ethical test preparation practices
- What parents and students need to know about standardized tests
- Implications for teachers

Recommended Activities to Complete (check the ones you plan to do)

- ❏ Activity 13.1: Standardized Tests Used in Your District, pp. 389–390
- ❏ Activity 13.2: A Definitions Pretest, p. 390
- ❏ Activity 13.3: Hills' Handy Hints, p. 399
- ❏ Activity 13.4: Interpret Your Own Standardized Test Report, p. 409
- ❏ Activity 13.5: Use Item Formulas to Help Students Learn, p. 412
- ❏ Activity 13.6: Translate Standardized Test Jargon into Student-Friendly Language, p. 414
- ❏ Activity 13.7: When Grades Don't Match the State Assessment Results, p. 427
- ❏ Activity 13.8: A Definitions Posttest, p. 428
- ❏ Try one idea from Chapter 13 with students. Summarize your and their reactions to the experience.
- ❏ Select portfolio entries.
- ❏ Plan for sharing your portfolio.

- ❏ Other: _____

_____

_____

_____

_____

3

Next Meeting Date: _____   **Time:** _____

Location: _____   **Bring:** _____

Chapter 13

Practical Help with Standardized Tests

Main Points

- Important definitions and common misconceptions
- How standardized tests are developed; what test scores mean
- Measurement error
- Using standardized tests to promote learning
- Ethical test preparation practices
- What parents and students need to know about standardized tests
- Implications for teachers

CASL DVD Segment

"Ethical Test Preparation" (5:10)

Judy Arter distinguishes between appropriate and inappropriate ways to help students prepare for upcoming standardized tests.

Agenda Options for Meeting 13

Discussion of Chapter 13 Reading and Activities.

- Short, open-ended reaction time to information in text.
- Discuss conclusions participants drew from homework activities.
- Watch and discuss the DVD segment, "Ethical Test Preparation."
- You may also want to conduct Activity 13.4, Activity 13.5, Activity 13.6, or Activity 13.7 as a whole-team activity during this meeting.
- Short discussion of which artifacts, if any, from this reading to place in participants' professional portfolios. You may wish to refer them to "Indicators of Sound Classroom Assessment Practice" from Chapter 1, page 27, as a guide for selecting artifacts.

Between Meetings: Recommended Activities to Complete Between Meetings 13 and 14

Suggest that participants do the following:

- Activity 2.5 "Where Am I Now? Self-Assessment," pages 50–51 again. Compare your results to the first time you did it. Answer the following questions: What do you notice? What has changed? Why do you think this occurred?

- Read "Closing Comments from the Authors," pages 431–435. Think about what your next steps in learning about assessment are. Write them down and include them in your portfolio.

- Prepare for portfolio sharing. You may want to read the suggestions for preparing your portfolio on page 429.

3

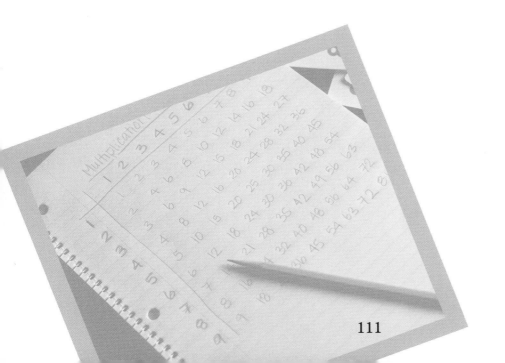

Meeting 14

Closure and Next Steps*

The text that follows is written for learning team members. We include it here so that you can think about and plan for closure and next steps in advance. It is reproduced in Tab 4, because you may want to use it as a handout for your learning team to help them decide what their final meeting will look like.

We recommend that you culminate your learning with a final session in which each team member shares their growth portfolios. You can do this one of two (or more) ways. Each person spends an allotted amount of time sharing the contents of their growth portfolio and receiving questions and comments, or you read each person's portfolio silently for about half of the time and then ask questions and offer comments for the rest of the meeting.

The Showcase Presentation

If you would like to get together with other learning teams for a joint culminating meeting, for instance if several teams have been formed in your school or district, you may like the idea of a showcase presentation. A *showcase* is a presentation of projects, artifacts, and ideas representing participants' learning. It provides an opportunity for teams to share their best ideas. Preparing a showcase display consolidates your thinking about the procedure being showcased, provides opportunity to glean nifty ideas from each other, and celebrates the hard work everyone has done. Here is how the showcase presentation works.

To prepare for a showcase presentation, take your growth portfolio to your final learning team meeting. Spend a few minutes per person explaining your entries. The purpose here is to select one of the entries from all the entries in everyone's portfolios that your team would be willing to "showcase" at the large group meeting.

---

* *Adapted from Stiggins et al. (CD-ROM), 2004, n.p., by permission of Educational Testing Service.*

We recommend selecting an entry you all would like others to have the opportunity to see and understand. It can be the work of your whole group, of any combination of your group, or of one member. Planning the showcase presentation, however, will be a team effort, and the focus of your learning team meeting time.

The Showcase Process

Showcases are not formal presentations in which each team has 15 or so minutes to talk about their work to a seated audience. Rather, this is a walkabout in which one person will stay at the team's table and the rest will circulate to the other tables. It is self-pacing. Sometimes your team's representative might be chatting with a single person. Sometimes that person may be giving a short explanation to a small group. In any case, since multiple presentations occur simultaneously in the same room, the setup is not conducive to large-screen presentations or typical workshop-type activities. (Note: The same person does not have to remain at your team's table the whole time; you can trade off so that everyone gets a chance to see other offerings.)

What to Prepare

You can make your team's presentation as simple or as complex as you want. Teams sometimes prepare a backboard (4' x 4' or so) that contains a self-explanatory visual display of their work—a title, displays, and a brief explanation of what participants are looking at and why it is important. Teams can post such things as rubrics, samples of student work, examples of assessments used, a list of strategies for involving students, letters to parents, and learning targets converted to student-friendly language.

Supplemental pieces (handouts, a computer, a notebook, etc. as appropriate) can be placed on a table for browsing if participants want more information.

4

Resources for Learning Team Members

Purpose	To provide the resources team members will need to conduct, keep track of, and share their learning and its impact on their students' progress
Content	◇ Overview of Tab 4
	◇ Goals of the CASL program
	◇ Tracking your learning
	◇ Suggestions for portfolio sharing

4 Resources for Learning Team Members

Overview of Tab 4

In Tab 4 we provide the resources team members will need to conduct, keep track of, and share their learning and its impact on their students' progress. The text is written directly to the learning team members; you can copy it and distribute it to each team member either before or during the first team meeting (described in Tab 3).

We begin with a brief statement of the CASL program goals and the five keys to assessment quality (described in Tab 1). The rest of the tab consists of suggestions for the following:

- Tracking and sharing learning

- Completing a reflective journal

- Assembling a portfolio

- Noting changes in practice

- Conducting a showcase presentation at the conclusion of the learning team experience

Goals of the CASL Program

The book you are about to read, *Classroom Assessment* for *Student Learning: Doing It Right—Using It Well* (which we refer to as *CASL*), focuses on two big ideas: (1) how to assess accurately; (2) how to use assessment to increase motivation and achievement. We have developed five keys to assessment quality that must be in place for both of those things to happen. The five keys to quality are illustrated in Figure 4.1.

Figure 4.1   **Keys to Quality Classroom Assessment**

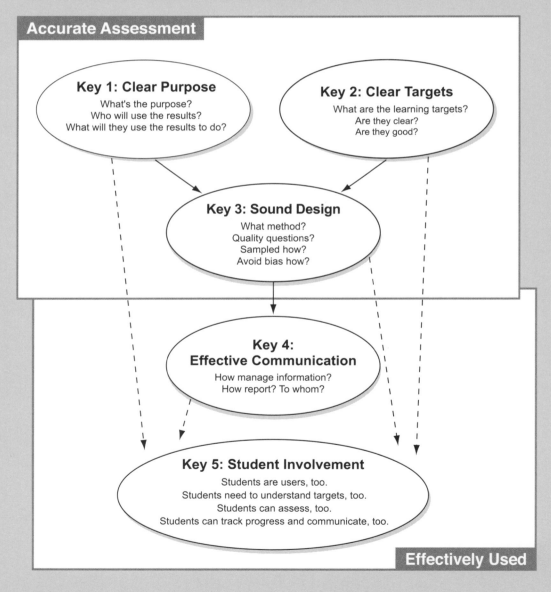

It follows that the goals for your study and application of the ideas also center on these five keys to quality. Figure 4.2 lays out the practices you will learn or refine through the study of *CASL*.

Figure 4.2   **Indicators of Sound Classroom Assesment Practice**

1 Clear Purposes Assessment processes and results serve clear and appropriate purposes.	• Teachers understand who the users and uses of classroom assessment information are and know their information needs. • Teachers understand the relationship between assessment and student motivation and craft assessment experiences to maximize motivation. • Teachers use classroom assessment processes and results formatively (assessment *for* learning). • Teachers use classroom assessment results summatively (assessment *of* learning) to inform someone beyond the classroom about students' achievement as of a particular point in time. • Teachers have a comprehensive plan over time for integrating assessment *for* and *of* learning in the classroom.
2 Clear Targets Assessment reflects clear and valued student learning targets.	• Teachers have clear learning targets for students; they know how to turn broad statements of content standards into classroom-level targets. • Teachers understand the various types of learning targets they hold for students. • Teachers select learning targets focused on the most important things students need to know and be able to do. • Teachers have a comprehensive plan over time for assessing learning targets.

Figure 4.2 *(continued)*

3 **Sound Design**	• Teachers understand what the various assessment methods are.
Learning targets are translated into assessments that yield accurate results.	• Teachers choose assessment methods that match intended learning targets.
	• Teachers design assessments that serve intended purposes.
	• Teachers sample learning appropriately in their assessments.
	• Teachers write assessment questions of all types well.
	• Teachers avoid sources of mismeasurement that bias results.

4 **Effective Communication**	• Teachers record assessment information accurately, keep it confidential, and appropriately combine and summarize it for reporting (including grades). Such summary accurately reflects current level of student learning.
Assessment results are managed well and communicated effectively.	• Teachers select the best reporting option (grades, narratives, portfolios, conferences) for each context (learning targets and intended users).
	• Teachers interpret and use standardized test results correctly.
	• Teachers effectively communicate assessment results to students.
	• Teachers effectively communicate assessment results to a variety of audiences outside the classroom, including parents, colleagues, and other stakeholders.

5 **Student Involvement**	• Teachers make learning targets clear to students.
Students are involved in their own assessment.	• Teachers involve students in assessing, tracking, and setting goals for their own learning.
	• Teachers involve students in communicating about their own learning.

Source: Adapted from Classroom Assessment *for* Student Learning: Doing It Right—Using It Well *(p. 27), by R. Stiggins, J. Arter, J. Chappuis, & S. Chappuis, 2004, Portland, OR: Assessment Training Institute. Copyright 2006, 2004 by Educational Testing Service. Adapted by permission.*

Tracking Your Learning*

Many people find it helpful to keep a record of their thoughts and questions as they read each chapter and try out activities, both for their own learning and to prepare themselves for learning team discussions.

Figure 4.3, found on page 128, represents an example of a reflective journal page, which you can copy as is or alter to suit your preferences.

We encourage you to collect evidence of your progress throughout your learning team experience and recommend that you assemble those artifacts into a growth portfolio. We call it a *growth* portfolio because its overriding intent is to show your growth in classroom assessment literacy.

> If you have not assembled a portfolio before, read (or skim) *CASL* Chapter 11 "Portfolios" first to make the process go smoothly.

Focusing Your Portfolio

You may not want to select items that illustrate *everything* you have learned—you may want to narrow your focus. Each *CASL* chapter will have specific recommendations for portfolio entries. Decide which activities to complete and/or to include based on your own personal learning goals. You may be focused on improving performance assessment in your classroom, in which case you will select portfolio entries to reflect your growth in that area. You may be most intrigued by the student-focused ideas presented and want

4

---

* *Adapted from Stiggins et al. (CD-ROM), 2004 (n.p.), by permission of Educational Testing Service.*

to create a portfolio that shows what you have done to involve students in assessment *for* learning. Use Figure 4.2 as a guide to identify which learning targets your portfolio will address.

Working Folders

The working folder is a collection of all the activities you complete, from which you will choose portfolio artifacts. Keep all the activities you complete. You never know when you will want to refer to something you did earlier, and your focus may change during your course of study, so you may decide later to include those artifacts.

Artifacts

Include in your portfolio your responses to Figure 4.4, "Classroom Assessment Confidence Questionnaire," found on pages 129–133.

Evaluate classroom assessments for quality using the rubrics in Figure 4.5, found on pages 134–138.

Use Figure 4.6, found on page 139, to record your evaluations of classroom assessments.

You may want to begin your portfolio with Figure 4.4, "Classroom Assessment Confidence Questionnaire," found on pages 129–133, because it establishes a baseline to which you can return periodically throughout your study. Retaking the questionnaire at the end of each of the three sections of the book will provide information you can use to reflect on the progress of your learning.

If you are completing a reflective journal, you can include some or all of the pages that demonstrate an aha! moment, the process you used to work through a difficult problem, or issues you still want to address.

We encourage you to include evidence of your ability to create and select accurate assessments in part by periodically evaluating assessments you use for quality. Figure 4.5, found on pages 134–138, presents an updated version of "Assessment Quality Rubrics" on the *CASL* CD-ROM. Figure 4.6, found on page 139, offers a form on which you may record your judgments about individual assessments.

Your Portfolio's Focus

Whatever you choose for your portfolio, we recommend that it show your growth in both of the central concepts: assessment accuracy and effective use, the "doing it right" and "using it well" of the book's title. All of our suggestions for portfolio entries are aimed at one or both of these targets.

Also consider collecting evidence of increased student motivation and achievement that you believe is attributable to changes in your assessment practice. Figure 4.7, found on pages 140–147, presents two versions of a student questionnaire—one for elementary students and one for middle school/high school students. Each version has two forms—a "pre" and a "post." Only the instructions differ between the "pre" and "post" forms; the questions remain the same. This is so you can use the questionnaire with students at the beginning of your study and then again at the end of the school year to determine your impact on their attitudes about and understanding of assessment information.

If you want to gather evidence to document students' changes in achievement, collect samples of their work from the beginning of your study and periodically throughout the year to look for changes. If you teach a large number of students, or if you teach a number of subjects, you may want to focus on a handful of students—one or more strong learners, midrange learners, and struggling learners. Save these samples and include them in your portfolio. These artifacts can be the most powerful testament to your learning, as student growth is the ultimate goal of your work.

Refer to Figure 4.2 for a list of CASL program learning targets.

Use Figure 4.8, found on page 148, as a cover sheet for each portfolio entry.

Annotations

Date each portfolio entry and make a note of which of your own selected learning targets it illustrates. Also include a comment indicating why you chose the item and what it shows. Figure 4.8, found on page 148, asks for this information and is designed to be attached to each entry.

Suggestions for Portfolio Sharing*

We recommend that you culminate your learning with a final session in which team members share their growth portfolios. You can do this one of two (or more) ways. Each person spends an allotted amount of time sharing portfolio contents and receiving questions and comments, or you read each person's portfolio silently for about half of the time and then ask questions and offer comments for the rest of the meeting.

Preparing to Share Your Portfolio**

Prepare to share your portfolio with your learning team or other audiences by doing one or both of the following activities.

1. Write an overall self-reflection on your learning. You may want to use one or more of the questions that follow to focus your reflection. Additionally, you may find that one or more of the forms designated for student portfolio use in Chapter 12 will help guide your reflection.

    *   What specific evidence of improvement do you see in your own classroom assessments? Comment on your proficiency in using as many different assessment methods as are relevant in your classroom. What criteria did you use to judge the quality of assessments? Make this clear to the reader.

    *   Did the nature and quality of your critiques change over time? Share evidence of this.

    *   What are you doing differently in the classroom as a result of what you have learned? How do these changes relate to the Five Keys to Quality Assessment? (Refer to Figure 4.2 if needed.)

    *   How has your thinking about assessment changed?

---

* *Adapted (except following subsection as noted) from Stiggins et al. (CD-ROM), 2004, n.p., by permission of Educational Testing Service.*

** *Adapted from Stiggins et al., 2004, pp. 429–430, by permission of Educational Testing Service.*

- Did your self-ratings of confidence change over time? In what specific ways?

- What has been the impact on students of assessment practices you have instituted as a part of this study?

- What questions did you begin this study with that you now can answer? What new questions do you have?

2. Write a "Dear Reader" letter, in which you tell your portfolio audience about yourself as a classroom assessor and point out what you would like your audience to notice about your portfolio. Be sure to include a statement of purpose for your portfolio.

Include a table of contents of all of the pieces in your portfolio. Organize your portfolio in a way that makes it easy for the reader to see your growth as a classroom assessor. Date everything, and for each piece, state why you included it and what evidence it provides.

Conduct your last team meeting as a celebration of learning by sharing your portfolios with one another. Congratulate each other and thank your team for their contribution to your learning.

The Showcase Presentation

If you would like to get together with other learning teams for a joint culminating meeting, for instance if several teams have been formed in your school or district, you may like the idea of a showcase presentation. A *showcase* is a presentation of projects, artifacts, and ideas representing participants' learning. It provides an opportunity for teams to share their best ideas. Preparing a showcase display consolidates your thinking about the procedure being showcased, provides opportunities to glean nifty ideas from each other, and celebrates the hard work everyone has done. Here is how the showcase presentation works.

To prepare for a showcase presentation, take your growth portfolio to your final learning team meeting. Spend a few minutes per person explaining your entries. The purpose here is to select one of the entries from all the entries in everyone's portfolios that your team would be willing to "showcase" at the large group meeting.

We recommend selecting an entry you all would like others to have the opportunity to see and understand. It can be the work of your whole group, of any combination of your group, or of one member. Planning the showcase presentation, however, will be a team effort, and the focus of your learning team meeting time.

The Showcase Process

Mixing It Up
During a showcase, the same person does not have to remain at your team's table the whole time; you can trade off so that everyone gets a chance to see other offerings.

A showcase is not a formal presentation in which each team has 15 or so minutes to talk about their work to a seated audience. Rather, this is a walkabout in which one person will stay at the team's table and the rest will circulate to the other tables. It is self-pacing. Sometimes your team's representative might be chatting with a single person. Sometimes that person may be giving a short explanation to a small group. In any case, since multiple presentations occur simultaneously in the same room, the setup is not conducive to large-screen presentations or typical workshop-type activities.

4

What to Prepare

You can make your team's presentation as simple or as complex as you want. Teams sometimes prepare a backboard (4' x 4' or so) that contains a self-explanatory visual display of their work—a title, displays, and a brief explanation of what participants are looking at and why it is important. Teams can post such things as rubrics, samples of student work, examples of assessments used, a list of strategies for involving students, letters to parents, and learning targets converted to student-friendly language.

Supplemental pieces (handouts, a computer, a notebook, etc. as appropriate) can be placed on a table for browsing if participants want more information.

4

Figure 4.3   **Reflective Journal**

Classroom Assessment* for *Student Learning: Doing It Right—Using It Well

Reflective Journal

Date:

Chapter: Pages read:

Thoughts, questions, reactions to what I read:

Activity(ies) tried:

Observations, questions, possible revisions to what I tried:

Figure 4.4 **Classroom Assessment Confidence Questionnaire**

Complete the questionnaire by circling the numbers that correspond to your answers to each question.

A. Clear Purpose.

I am confident of the following:

	I'm uncertain about my confidence	I'm not very confident	I'm somewhat confident	I'm very confident
1. I understand the various users of classroom assessment information, including students, and can accommodate their various assessment *for* and *of* learning needs.	?	0	1	2
2. I understand the relationship between assessment and student motivation and consciously use assessment to motivate students to want to learn.	?	0	1	2
3. I balance assessment *for* and *of* learning in my classroom and have a plan for integrating them over time.	?	0	1	2
4. I use classroom assessment information to guide and revise teaching.	?	0	1	2

4

Figure 4.4   (continued)

B. Clear Targets.

I can clearly describe the learning targets I want my students to hit. I have done the following:

	I'm uncertain if I've done this yet	I haven't done this yet	I've started	I'm well on the way
1. Outlined in writing the **subject matter content knowledge** my students are to master.	?	0	1	2
2. Differentiated content students are to **learn outright** from content they are to **learn to retrieve** later through the use of references.	?	0	1	2
3. Defined in writing the specific **patterns of reasoning** students are to master.	?	0	1	2
4. Articulated in writing the performance skills **I expect students** to learn to demonstrate (where it is the actual doing that counts).	?	0	1	2
5. Defined the key attributes of **products** I expect students to learn to create.	?	0	1	2
6. Thought through and defined **academic dispositions** (school-related attitudes) I hope my students will develop.	?	0	1	2
7. Considered whether there's anything about my learning targets or how they are written that will be unclear to any of my students.	?	0	1	2
8. Met with other teachers across grade levels to merge my expectations into a **continuous-progress curriculum**.	?	0	1	2

Figure 4.4   (continued)

C. Sound Design.

I can translate my learning targets for students and purposes for assessment into dependable assessments that yield accurate results. I am confident of the following:

	I'm uncertain about my confidence	I'm not very confident	I'm somewhat confident	I'm very confident
1. I can define key standards of assessment quality in common-sense, understandable terms.	?	0	1	2
2. I can develop high-quality **selected response/short answer assessments** (multiple choice, true/false, matching, fill in).	?	0	1	2
3. I can develop high-quality **extended written response assessments**.	?	0	1	2
4. I can develop high-quality **performance assessments** (observation and judgment).	?	0	1	2
5. I can develop high-quality **personal communication-based assessments** (interviews, oral exams, etc.).	?	0	1	2
6. I can select among assessment types based on target type and purpose.	?	0	1	2
7. I can sample appropriately and avoid sources of bias and distortion.	?	0	1	2

Figure 4.4   (continued)

D. Effective Communication.

I am confident of the following:

	I'm uncertain about my confidence	I'm not very confident	I'm somewhat confident	I'm very confident
1. I understand and can apply *principles of effective communication* about student achievement.	?	0	1	2
2. I provide more descriptive feedback than evaluative feedback to students.	?	0	1	2
3. I can record and combine assessment information to accurately reflect student learning.	?	0	1	2
4. I can use *report card grades* to communicate accurately and effectively.	?	0	1	2
5. I can use *other written report cards* to communicate accurately and effectively.	?	0	1	2
6. I can use *portfolios* to communicate accurately and effectively.	?	0	1	2
7. I can use *parent-teacher conferences* to communicate accurately and effectively.	?	0	1	2
8. I can use *student-involved conferences* to communicate accurately and effectively.	?	0	1	2
9. I can understand and use the results of *standardized achievement tests*.	?	0	1	2

Figure 4.4 (continued)

E. Student Involvement.

I turn assessment procedures and information into instructional interventions in the following ways:

	I'm uncertain about my confidence	I'm not very confident	I'm somewhat confident	I'm very confident
1. I make learning targets clear to students.	?	0	1	2
2. My students can describe what learning targets they are to achieve.	?	0	1	2
3. I give students opportunities to self-assess and set goals for further learning.	?	0	1	2
4. I give students opportunities to reflect on and share their learning progress with others.	?	0	1	2
5. I give students opportunities to provide input on assessment design.	?	0	1	2

F. Final Reflections

1. I have the most skill and confidence in the following assessment areas:

2. I want to work most on the following assessment skills:

Source: Adapted from Classroom Assessment *for* Student Learning: Doing It Right—Using It Well *(CD-ROM, n.p.), by R. Stiggins, J. Arter., J. Chappuis, & S. Chappuis, 2004, Portland, OR: Assessment Training Institute. Copyright 2006, 2004 by Educational Testing Service. Adapted by permission.*

Figure 4.5 **Rubric for Evaluating Classroom Assessments for Quality**

KEY 1: CLEAR PURPOSES		
5 = Ready to Use	**3 = On Its Way**	**1 = Needs Significant Work**
• The intended users and uses are identified. • It is clear how the intended use fits into an overall plan that includes both assessments *for* and *of* learning over time.	• The intended users and uses can be inferred. • How the intended use fits into an overall plan that includes both assessments *for* and *of* learning is not stated, but can be inferred.	• The intended users and uses are not identified and cannot be accurately inferred. • It is difficult to tell how the intended use fits into an overall plan that includes both assessments *for* and *of* learning.

KEY 2: CLEAR TARGETS		
5 = Ready to Use	**3 = On Its Way**	**1 = Needs Significant Work**
• Learning targets measured by the assessment are stated. • The learning targets are clear. • The match between stated learning targets and what is on the assessment is clear. • Learning targets are clearly connected to the state/provincial/district content standards.	• Learning targets measured by the assessment are stated or can be inferred easily from the assessment. • Learning targets may be somewhat unclear. • There is a partial match between stated learning targets and what is on the assessment. • Learning targets are partially or loosely connected to the state/provincial/district content standards.	• Learning targets measured by the assessment are not stated and cannot be accurately inferred. • Learning targets are stated, but vague or unclear. • There is no apparent match between stated learning targets and what is on the assessment. • There is no apparent connection between learning targets and the state/provincial/district content standards.

Figure 4.5   (continued)

KEY 3: SOUND DESIGN Selecting an Assessment Method		
5 = Ready to Use	**3 = On Its Way**	**1 = Needs Significant Work**
• The method(s) chosen is/are capable of accurately reflecting the learning target(s) to be assessed.	• When multiple methods are used in an assessment, sometimes the proper method is selected; sometimes an improper method is used.	• The method(s) used is/are not capable of accurately reflecting the learning targets(s) in question.

KEY 3: SOUND DESIGN Sampling		
5 = Ready to Use	**3 = On Its Way**	**1 = Needs Significant Work**
• The learning targets tested represent what was taught. (In the case of diagnostic assessment, they represent what is intended to be taught.) • The relative importance of each learning target on the assessment matches the relative importance given to it during instruction. • The sample size is large enough to inform the decisions intended to be made, or it is clear that it is part of a larger plan to gather enough information over time.	• The learning targets tested partially represent what was taught. (In the case of diagnostic assessment, they partially represent what is intended to be taught.) • The relative importance of each learning target on the assessment partially matches the relative importance given to it during instruction.	• The learning targets tested do not represent what was taught. (In the case of diagnostic assessment, they do not represent what is intended to be taught.) • The relative importance of each learning target on the assessment does not match the relative importance given to it during instruction. • The sample size is not large enough or is substantially greater than needed to inform the decisions intended to be made.

Figure 4.5   (continued)

KEY 3: SOUND DESIGN Item Quality		
5 = Ready to Use	**3 = On Its Way**	**1 = Needs Significant Work**
• Selected response and short answer items adhere to standards of quality (See *CASL* pp. 138–146). • Extended written response items adhere to standards of quality (See *CASL* pp. 174–177). • Extended written response scoring procedures adhere to guidelines for quality (See *CASL* pp. 177–179). • Performance assessment tasks adhere to standards of quality (See *CASL* pp. 218–229). • Performance assessment scoring guides/rubrics adhere to guidelines for quality (*CASL* pp. 200–218). • Oral examination assessments adhere to guidelines for quality (See *CASL* p. 265).	• Selected response and short answer items partially adhere to standards of quality. • Extended written response items partially adhere to standards of quality. • Extended written response scoring procedures partially adhere to guidelines for quality. • Performance assessment tasks partially adhere to standards of quality. • Performance assessment scoring guides/rubrics partially adhere to guidelines for quality. • Oral examination assessments partially adhere to guidelines for quality.	• Selected response and short answer items do not adhere to standards of quality. • Extended written response items do not adhere to standards of quality. • Extended written response scoring procedures do not adhere to guidelines for quality. • Performance assessment tasks do not adhere to standards of quality. • Performance assessment scoring guides/rubrics do not adhere to guidelines for quality. • Oral examination assessments do not adhere to guidelines for quality.

4

Figure 4.5   (continued)

KEY 3: SOUND DESIGN Bias and Distortion		
5 = Ready to Use	**3 = On Its Way**	**1 = Needs Significant Work**
• There is nothing in the assessment itself or in the conditions under which it is administered that could lead to inaccurate estimates of student learning (See *CASL* pp. 114–116). • Accommodations made for diverse student characteristics do not result in any distortions in the final judgment of student learning. • Instructions are present, clear, and concise.	• There are a few things in the assessment itself or in the conditions under which it is administered that could lead to inaccurate estimates of student learning. • Accommodations made for diverse student characteristics may result in slight distortions in the final judgment of student learning. • Instructions are present, but not as clear or concise as they could be.	• There are many things in the assessment itself or in the conditions under which it is administered that could lead to inaccurate estimates of student learning. • Accommodations made for diverse student characteristics will result in distortions in the final judgment of student learning. • Instructions are not present, or are difficult to follow.

KEY 4: EFFECTIVE COMMUNICATION		
5 = Ready to Use	**3 = On Its Way**	**1 = Needs Significant Work**
• Results from the assessment are communicated in a timely manner. • Results from the assessment are communicated so that the intended users of the information understand what they mean and how they connect to learning. • Results provide clear direction for what to do next.	• Results from the assessment are communicated so that the intended users of the information may have questions about what they mean or how they connect to learning. • Results do not provide entirely clear direction for what to do next.	• Results from the assessment are not communicated in a timely manner. • Results from the assessment are not communicated so that the intended users of the information understand what they mean or how they connect to learning. • Results do not provide direction for what to do next.

Figure 4.5   (continued)

KEY 5: STUDENT INVOLVEMENT		
5 = Ready to Use	**3 = On Its Way**	**1 = Needs Significant Work**
• When appropriate, learning targets are written in terms that students can clearly understand. • When appropriate, students are involved in the assessment process. • When appropriate, the assessment is designed so that students can use the results to identify specific strengths and weaknesses, and to set meaningful goals for further learning. • There is a mechanism in place for students to track their own progress on learning targets and to participate in communicating their status to others, if appropriate for the context.	• Learning targets would be somewhat unclear to students, but could be revised to be clear. • Student are minimally involved in the assessment process, when it would be appropriate to do so. • The assessment design would need some work for students to be able to use it easily to identify specific strengths and weaknesses, and to set meaningful goals for further learning. • There is some assistance for students in tracking progress and communicating progress, but either it has to be inferred, or it is not complete.	• Learning targets would have to be entirely rewritten so that students could understand them. • Students are not involved in the assessment process, when it would be appropriate to do so. • Students cannot use the assessment results to identify specific strengths and weaknesses, or to set meaningful goals for further learning. • There is not a mechanism in place for students to track their own progress on learning targets and to participate in communicating their status to others, when it is appropriate for the context.

Source: Adapted from Classroom Assessment *for* Student Learning: Doing It Right—Using It Well *(CD-ROM, n.p.),*
by R. Stiggins, J. Arter., J. Chappuis, & S. Chappuis, 2004, Portland, OR: Assessment Training Institute.
Copyright 2006, 2004 by Educational Testing Service. Adapted by permission.

Figure 4.6 **Assessment Evaluation Form**

Use this form to record your evaluation of assessments you give.

Title of Assessment: _____   Date Given: _____

Date Evaluated: _____

Key to Quality	Judgment	Reasons
1. Clear Purpose		
2. Clear Targets		
3. Sound Design • Selecting Method		
• Sampling		
• Item Quality		
• Bias and Distortion		
4. Effective Communication		
5. Student Involvement		

Changes to make in this assessment:

Figure 4.7 **Student Questionnaires**

Assessment FOR Learning
ELEMENTARY SCHOOL STUDENT SURVEY

PRE

INSTRUCTION TO STUDENTS:

Today you are going to complete a questionnaire to help me know more about some of your experiences in school. The answers will be anonymous. That means that no one but you will know what you said. You will not put your name on the questionnaire. Your honest answers will help me make important decisions about what works best for our class.

Please fill in the bubble completely.

	Not True	Sometimes True	Often True	Always True
1. I can learn whatever I need to learn to succeed in school.	○	○	○	○
2. After we take a test, we use it to show us what we are good at and what we still need to work on.	○	○	○	○
3. I know if my work is good or not before I give it to the teacher.	○	○	○	○
4. I can tell what I need to do to make my work better.	○	○	○	○
5. When I try to learn something hard, I can learn it.	○	○	○	○
6. I can use samples of my work to show what I have learned.	○	○	○	○
7. I keep track of how my work gets better over time.	○	○	○	○
8. My teacher uses examples of good and poor work to help me understand what good work looks like.	○	○	○	○

TURN THE PAGE OVER FOR MORE QUESTIONS →   1

Figure 4.7 (continued)

	Not True	Sometimes True	Often True	Always True
9. It is clear to me what I am expected to learn.	○	○	○	○
10. My teacher tells our class what we are going to learn before we start to learn it.	○	○	○	○
11. I can explain why my work is good or not.	○	○	○	○
12. I know how to do work that will get a good grade.	○	○	○	○
13. If I decide to get good grades, I really can do it.	○	○	○	○
14. My teacher's system of grading is clear to me.	○	○	○	○
15. I do well in school.	○	○	○	○
16. I can compare samples of my work to show how much I have improved.	○	○	○	○
17. My teacher helps us judge the quality of our work before we turn it in.	○	○	○	○
18. I am good at learning.	○	○	○	○
19. After learning something, I can explain what I learned.	○	○	○	○

20. What are the main reasons students get good grades?

They are lucky.	They get along with the teacher.	They produce good work.
○	○	○

21. When students manage to learn hard things in school, what is the main reason?

They are lucky.	They get along with the teacher.	They produce good work.
○	○	○

THANK YOU!

4

2

Source: Created by Educational Testing Service in partnership with Battelle for Kids, Columbus, OH. Copyright © 2006 Educational Testing Service. Reprinted by permission.

Figure 4.7   (continued)

Assessment FOR Learning
ELEMENTARY SCHOOL STUDENT SURVEY

POST

INSTRUCTION TO STUDENTS:
Today you are going to complete a questionnaire. It is the same one you completed earlier this year. The answers will be anonymous. That means that no one but you will know what you said. You will not put your name on the questionnaire. Your honest answers will help me evaluate teaching practices I have been using this year with you.

Please fill in the bubble completely.

	Not True	Sometimes True	Often True	Always True
1. I can learn whatever I need to learn to succeed in school.	○	○	○	○
2. After we take a test, we use it to show us what we are good at and what we still need to work on.	○	○	○	○
3. I know if my work is good or not before I give it to the teacher.	○	○	○	○
4. I can tell what I need to do to make my work better.	○	○	○	○
5. When I try to learn something hard, I can learn it.	○	○	○	○
6. I can use samples of my work to show what I have learned.	○	○	○	○
7. I keep track of how my work gets better over time.	○	○	○	○
8. My teacher uses examples of good and poor work to help me understand what good work looks like.	○	○	○	○

TURN THE PAGE OVER FOR MORE QUESTIONS →   **1**

Figure 4.7   (continued)

	Not True	Sometimes True	Often True	Always True
9. It is clear to me what I am expected to learn.	◯	◯	◯	◯
10. My teacher tells our class what we are going to learn before we start to learn it.	◯	◯	◯	◯
11. I can explain why my work is good or not.	◯	◯	◯	◯
12. I know how to do work that will get a good grade.	◯	◯	◯	◯
13. If I decide to get good grades, I really can do it.	◯	◯	◯	◯
14. My teacher's system of grading is clear to me.	◯	◯	◯	◯
15. I do well in school.	◯	◯	◯	◯
16. I can compare samples of my work to show how much I have improved.	◯	◯	◯	◯
17. My teacher helps us judge the quality of our work before we turn it in.	◯	◯	◯	◯
18. I am good at learning.	◯	◯	◯	◯
19. After learning something, I can explain what I learned.	◯	◯	◯	◯

20. What are the main reasons students get good grades?

They are lucky.	They get along with the teacher.	They produce good work.
◯	◯	◯

21. When students manage to learn hard things in school, what is the main reason?

They are lucky.	They get along with the teacher.	They produce good work.
◯	◯	◯

THANK YOU!   2

Source: Created by Educational Testing Service in partnership with Battelle for Kids, Columbus, OH.
Copyright © 2006 Educational Testing Service. Reprinted by permission.

Figure 4.7   (continued)

Assessment FOR Learning
MIDDLE/HIGH SCHOOL STUDENT SURVEY

PRE

INSTRUCTION TO STUDENTS:

Today you are going to complete a questionnaire to help me know more about some of your experiences in school. The answers will be anonymous—you won't put your name on the questionnaire. Your information will be combined with other students' responses to help determine the effectiveness of certain teaching strategies.

For each number, you will see a statement, then five bubbles, and then another statement.
1. Read both statements first.
2. Decide which one you agree with most closely.

If you strongly agree with one statement or the other, fill in the "Strongly Agree" bubble closest to the statement you agree with.

If you somewhat agree, fill in the "Agree" bubble closest to the statement you agree with.

If you could go either way or if each statement applies to your situation equally, fill in the "Uncertain" bubble.

Fill in the bubble completely. Please let me know now if you have any questions.

	Strongly Agree	Agree	Uncertain	Agree	Strongly Agree	
1. I can explain why my work is good or not.	○	○	○	○	○	I cannot explain why my work is good or not.
2. I do not have opportunities to use tests to determine what I have learned and what I still need to work on.	○	○	○	○	○	I have regular opportunities to use tests to determine what I have learned and what I still need to work on.
3. I can learn whatever I need to learn to succeed in this subject.	○	○	○	○	○	I cannot learn what I need to succeed in this subject.
4. The grade I get depends on what my teacher does.	○	○	○	○	○	The grade I get depends mainly on the quality of the work I do.
5. Last year in this subject, my grades were low.	○	○	○	○	○	Last year in this subject, my grades were high.
6. I am not good at learning.	○	○	○	○	○	I am good at learning.

TURN THE PAGE OVER FOR MORE QUESTIONS →   **1**

Figure 4.7 (continued)

	Strongly Agree	Agree	Uncertain	Agree	Strongly Agree	
7. Even if I decide to get good grades, I cannot do it.	○	○	○	○	○	If I decide to get good grades, I really can do it.
8. I am good at evaluating the quality of my work.	○	○	○	○	○	I do not know if my work is good until the teacher evaluates it.
9. I understand the learning targets I am expected to learn in this class.	○	○	○	○	○	I do not understand the learning targets I am expected to learn in this class.
10. I track my improvement in learning.	○	○	○	○	○	I do not track my improvement in learning.
11. I would have a hard time describing what I have learned.	○	○	○	○	○	I can describe what I have learned.
12. The teacher's system of grading is not clear to me.	○	○	○	○	○	The teacher's system of grading is clear to me.
13. I know how to produce the level of quality that is expected to get a good grade.	○	○	○	○	○	I do not know how to produce the level of quality that is expected to get a good grade.
14. I can compare samples of my work to show how much I have improved.	○	○	○	○	○	I cannot compare samples of my work to show how much I have improved.
15. The grade I get depends mainly on luck.	○	○	○	○	○	The grade I get depends mainly on the quality of the work I do.
16. My teacher provides examples of strong and weak work to help me understand what is expected.	○	○	○	○	○	My teacher does not provide examples of strong and weak work to help me understand what is expected.
17. The teacher is the only one who judges the quality of my work.	○	○	○	○	○	I have regular opportunities to judge the quality of my own work.
18. When I try to learn something hard, I can learn it.	○	○	○	○	○	When I try to learn something hard, I cannot learn it.
19. I am good at using tests to determine what I have learned and what I still need to work on.	○	○	○	○	○	Tests do not help me see what I have learned and what I still need to work on.
20. It is clear to me what learning targets I am to learn.	○	○	○	○	○	I am not sure what learning targets I am responsible for learning.
21. I can use samples of my work to show what I have learned.	○	○	○	○	○	I cannot use samples of my work to show what I have learned.

THANK YOU!   **2**

Source: Created by Educational Testing Service in partnership with Battelle for Kids, Columbus, OH. Copyright © 2006 Educational Testing Service. Reprinted by permission.

Figure 4.7   (continued)

Assessment FOR Learning
MIDDLE/HIGH SCHOOL STUDENT SURVEY

POST

INSTRUCTION TO STUDENTS:

Today you are going to complete a questionnaire. It is the same one you completed earlier this year. The answers will again be anonymous. This time, please *think only about your experiences in this class.* Your honest answers will help me evaluate teaching practices I have been using this year with you.

For each number, you will see a statement, then five bubbles, and then another statement.
1. Read both statements first.
2. Decide which one you agree with most closely.

If you strongly agree with one statement or the other, fill in the "Strongly Agree" bubble closest to the statement you agree with.

If you somewhat agree, fill in the "Agree" bubble closest to the statement you agree with.

If you could go either way or if each statement applies to your situation equally, fill in the "Uncertain" bubble.

Fill in the bubble completely. Please let me know now if you have any questions.

IN THIS CLASS:	Strongly Agree	Agree	Uncertain	Agree	Strongly Agree	
1. I can explain why my work is good or not.	O	O	O	O	O	I cannot explain why my work is good or not.
2. I do not have opportunities to use tests to determine what I have learned and what I still need to work on.	O	O	O	O	O	I have regular opportunities to use tests to determine what I have learned and what I still need to work on.
3. I can learn whatever I need to learn to succeed in this subject.	O	O	O	O	O	I cannot learn what I need to succeed in this subject.
4. The grade I get depends on what my teacher does.	O	O	O	O	O	The grade I get depends mainly on the quality of the work I do.
5. Last year in this subject, my grades were low.	O	O	O	O	O	Last year in this subject, my grades were high.
6. I am not good at learning.	O	O	O	O	O	I am good at learning.

TURN THE PAGE OVER FOR MORE QUESTIONS → 1

Figure 4.7 (continued)

	Strongly Agree	Agree	Uncertain	Agree	Strongly Agree	
7. Even if I decide to get good grades, I cannot do it.	○	○	○	○	○	If I decide to get good grades, I really can do it.
8. I am good at evaluating the quality of my work.	○	○	○	○	○	I do not know if my work is good until the teacher evaluates it.
9. I understand the learning targets I am expected to learn in this class.	○	○	○	○	○	I do not understand the learning targets I am expected to learn in this class.
10. I track my improvement in learning.	○	○	○	○	○	I do not track my improvement in learning.
11. I would have a hard time describing what I have learned.	○	○	○	○	○	I can describe what I have learned.
12. The teacher's system of grading is not clear to me.	○	○	○	○	○	The teacher's system of grading is clear to me.
13. I know how to produce the level of quality that is expected to get a good grade.	○	○	○	○	○	I do not know how to produce the level of quality that is expected to get a good grade.
14. I can compare samples of my work to show how much I have improved.	○	○	○	○	○	I cannot compare samples of my work to show how much I have improved.
15. The grade I get depends mainly on luck.	○	○	○	○	○	The grade I get depends mainly on the quality of the work I do.
16. My teacher provides examples of strong and weak work to help me understand what is expected.	○	○	○	○	○	My teacher does not provide examples of strong and weak work to help me understand what is expected.
17. The teacher is the only one who judges the quality of my work.	○	○	○	○	○	I have regular opportunities to judge the quality of my own work.
18. When I try to learn something hard, I can learn it.	○	○	○	○	○	When I try to learn something hard, I cannot learn it.
19. I am good at using tests to determine what I have learned and what I still need to work on.	○	○	○	○	○	Tests do not help me see what I have learned and what I still need to work on.
20. It is clear to me what learning targets I am to learn.	○	○	○	○	○	I am not sure what learning targets I am responsible for learning.
21. I can use samples of my work to show what I have learned.	○	○	○	○	○	I cannot use samples of my work to show what I have learned.

THANK YOU!   **2**

Source: Created by Educational Testing Service in partnership with Battelle for Kids, Columbus, OH. Copyright © 2006 Educational Testing Service. Reprinted by permission.

Figure 4.8   **Portfolio Entry Cover Sheet**

Date: _____

Title of selection: _____

Learning target(s) this selection addresses:

_____   Key 1: Clear Purpose

_____   Key 2: Clear Targets

_____   Key 3: Sound Design

_____   Key 4: Effective Communication

_____   Key 5: Student Involvement

What this selection illustrates about my learning/why I chose this selection:

Source: Adapted from Classroom Assessment *for* Student Learning: Doing It Right—Using It Well *(CD-ROM, n.p.), by R. Stiggins, J. Arter., J. Chappuis, & S. Chappuis, 2004, Portland, OR: Assessment Training Institute. Copyright 2006, 2004 by Educational Testing Service. Adapted by permission.*

5

Additional CASL
Program Resources

Purpose	To provide an in-depth look at other CASL program resources available and a picture of how they all fit together
Content	◇ Overview of Tab 5
	◇ Program books
	◇ Separate CASL program videos/DVDs
	◇ Journal articles
	◇ How CASL program resources interrelate

5 Additional CASL Program Resources

Overview of Tab 5

The CASL program offers a range of books and interactive training videos, all focused on improving assessment in the classroom. In this tab, we describe the products that comprise our program. A complete list of the book and CD/DVD titles appears in Figure 5.1. All books, videos, and DVDs are available from our website (http://www.ets.org/ati).

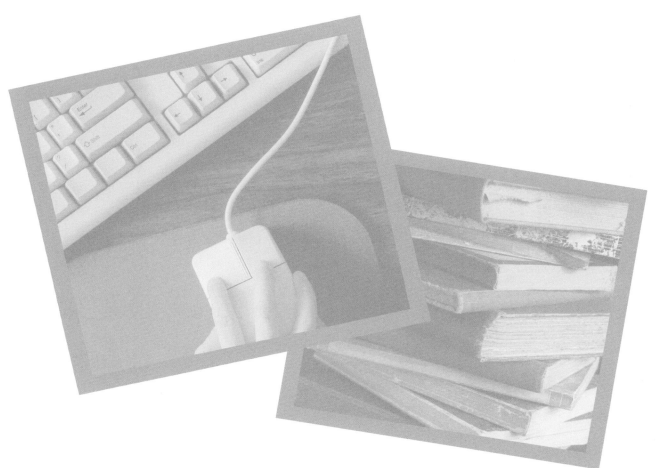

5

151

Figure 5.1 **Learning Team Resources: Professional Books and DVDs**

Books for Teachers, Administrators, and Parents

1. *Classroom Assessment* for *Student Learning: Doing It Right—Using It Well*
   - Accompanying CD, *Activities & Resources*
   - Accompanying DVD, *Demonstrations & Presentations*

2. *Assessment FOR Learning: An Action Guide for School Leaders*
   - Accompanying CD, *Assessment FOR Learning: Activities & Resources*
   - Accompanying DVD, *Assessment FOR Learning: A Hopeful Vision of the Future*

3. *Understanding School Assessment: A Parent and Community Guide to Helping Students Learn*

4. *Creating & Recognizing Quality Rubrics*
   - Accompanying CD

5. *A Repair Kit for Grading: 15 Fixes for Broken Grades*

Interactive Training Videos/DVDs

- *Assessment* for *Student Motivation*

- *Assessing Reasoning in the Classroom*

- *Evaluating Assessment Quality: Hands-On Practice*

- *Commonsense Paper and Pencil Assessments*

- *Designing Performance Assessments* for *Learning*

- *Grading & Reporting in Standards-Based Schools*

- *Student-Involved Conferences*

Other Products

Learning Team Facilitator Handbook: A Resource for Collaborative Study of Classroom Assessment *for* Student Learning (the present text)

New Mission, New Beliefs: Assessment for *Learning* (free DVD—order from http://www.ets.org/ati)

Program Books

Central Text

Classroom Assessment for *Student Learning: Doing It Right—Using It Well*
By Rick Stiggins, Judy Arter, Jan Chappuis, and Steve Chappuis

This essential book on assessment *for* learning is grounded in research that shows how student motivation and learning can improve with student-involved classroom assessment. It teaches both how to develop high-quality classroom assessments and how to use them in service of student achievement. This combination text and workbook features practical examples and expanded information about assessment *for* learning in everyday instruction. Written for individual use or group study.

Administrator Text

Assessment FOR Learning: An Action Guide for School Leaders
by Steve Chappuis, Rick Stiggins, Judy Arter, and Jan Chappuis

This book helps school administrators define a vision of what excellence in assessment looks like, and then charts the path to achieve that vision. The specific competencies leaders need to support assessment *for* learning are identified and amplified by activities and resources to help learn and apply the skills. Each book includes a DVD of Rick Stiggins presenting *Assessment FOR Learning: A Hopeful Vision of the Future* and a CD-ROM containing more than 40 individual and group activities, teaching resources, and planning tools. Written for individual use or group study.

5

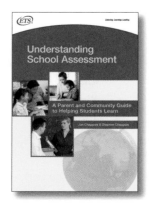

Parent and Community Text

Understanding School Assessment: A Parent and Community Guide to Helping Students Learn
by Jan Chappuis and Steve Chappuis

This book helps parents understand the role classroom assessment can play in improving student learning. Parents learn how to work with teachers, schools, districts, and other parents to ensure a quality school assessment environment. Comes with a study guide.

Supplementary Text for *CASL*

Creating & Recognizing Quality Rubrics
by Judith A. Arter and Jan Chappuis

Teachers learn to choose or develop sound instructional rubrics and to use rubrics effectively with students to maximize learning. An accompanying CD-ROM contains more than 25 sample rubrics. Recommended for use with the companion training video, *Designing Performance Assessments* for *Learning*.

Supplementary Text for *CASL*

A Repair Kit for Grading: 15 Fixes for Broken Grades
by Ken O'Connor

Classroom teachers and school and district leaders gain a deeper understanding of the issues involved in sound grading practices. O'Connor also provides practical strategies and alternatives to help change how students are graded.

5

Separate CASL Program Videos/DVDs

The ETS Classroom Assessment Professional Development Program is supported by seven separate interactive videos designed to correlate with specific content from *Classroom Assessment* for *Student Learning: Doing It Right—Using It Well*. Each video is formatted so that participants view a segment and then engage in a group discussion or activity. A user's guide on CD accompanies each video and includes printable handouts to guide discussions and activities. Many teams use one or more of these videos to extend their study of a particular chapter or chapters.

Assessment *for* Student Motivation (45:00)
CASL Chapter 2

In this video, Rick Stiggins explains why the behavior management model of rewards and punishments has not been a productive way to think about assessment. He then offers a new vision, explaining the relationships among student-involved assessment *for* learning, student confidence, and student achievement.

Assessing Reasoning in the Classroom (68:00)
CASL Chapters 3, 5, & 6

Rick Stiggins offers practical, effective ways to use assessments to teach reasoning and to help students succeed at problem solving.

5

Evaluating Assessment Quality: Hands-On Practice (36:00)

CASL Chapters 4, 5, & 6

The video begins with Rick Stiggins and Judy Arter teaching the standards of classroom assessment quality. Viewers are then given the opportunity to critique assessments against the standards of quality.

Commonsense Paper and Pencil Assessments (56:00)

CASL Chapter 5

Rick Stiggins shows how to design paper and pencil tests and shares strategies for using them to increase student motivation and achievement.

Designing Performance Assessments *for* **Learning** (75:00)

CASL Chapter 7

Judy Arter and Jan Chappuis show how to evaluate performance tasks and rubrics for quality. This video also includes a segment on how to develop a rubric, with examples taken from the work of a team of science teachers.

Grading & Reporting in Standards-Based Schools (60:00)

CASL Chapter 10

Rick Stiggins and Ken O'Connor guide viewers through a discussion of the most compelling issues related to collecting evidence of student achievement and lay out a process to develop more effective grading practices.

5

Student-Involved Conferences (60:00)

CASL Chapter 12

Anne Davies and Rick Stiggins share effective ways to prepare students to participate in conferences and describe keys to productive student-involved conferences. Viewers have the option of participating in a simulation of a student-led conference to translate the information into practice.

Journal Articles

On our website (http://www.ets.org/ati), you will find links to a collection of articles that describe various aspects of assessment quality, assessment *for* learning, and the learning team approach to professional development. Many people use one or more of the articles to introduce these ideas to their staffs.

Black, P., & Wiliam, D. 1998. Inside the black box: Raising standards through classroom assessment. *Phi Delta Kappan, 80*(2), 139–148.

> Paul Black and Dylan Wiliam offer a synthesis of research on the effects of formative assessment on student achievement. They describe improvements needed in classroom formative assessment practice and changes required in school district policy. They conclude with four steps to implementing effective formative assessment in the classroom.

Stiggins, R. J. 2004. New assessment beliefs for a new school mission. *Phi Delta Kappan, 86*(1), 22–27.

> We have inherited an assessment legacy that has actually prevented us from tapping the full power of assessment for school improvement, Rick Stiggins maintains. He offers a new vision of assessment that has the potential of bringing about remarkable gains in student achievement.

5

Stiggins, R. J. 2006. Assessment *for* learning: A key to motivation and achievement. *EDge, 2*(2), 1–20.

> Rick Stiggins describes a vision of a balanced assessment system that meets the needs of all decision makers and details what assessments *for* learning will do for student confidence, motivation, and achievement, as well as for school effectiveness.

Chappuis, J. 2005. Helping students understand assessment. *Educational Leadership, 63*(3), 39–43.

> Jan Chappuis summarizes the impact formative assessment practices can have on students' learning and then translates research recommendations into a series of specific actions teachers and students can take in the classroom. Called "Seven Strategies of Assessment *for* Learning," the actions allow teachers to identify and meet students' information needs about their own learning.

Stiggins, R. J., & Chappuis, J. 2006. What a difference a word makes: Assessment FOR learning rather than assessment OF learning helps students succeed. *Journal of Staff Development, 27*(1), 10–14.

> Rick Stiggins and Jan Chappuis explain the specific assessment competencies teachers need to master to help fulfill the potential of assessment *for* learning. They explain why common models of staff development are insufficient and show how the learning team approach to professional development can be used to help teachers polish classroom assessment practices.

5

How CASL Program Resources Interrelate

Part I: Principles of Assessment *for* Learning and Assessment Quality

CASL CHAPTER	VIDEO/DVD	RELATED BOOKS
Chapter 1 Overview of keys to quality classroom assessment	*New Mission, New Beliefs: Assessment for Learning*	*Understanding School Assessment: A Parent and Community Guide to Helping Students Learn*
Chapter 2 Balance; student motivation; assessment FOR learning	*Assessment for Student Motivation*	
Chapter 3 Clear learning targets	*Assessing Reasoning in the Classroom*	*Assessment FOR Learning: An Action Guide for School Leaders*

5

Part II: Assessment Methods

CASL CHAPTER	VIDEO/DVD	RELATED BOOKS
Chapter 4 Assessment methods; target–method match; test plans	*Evaluating Assessment Quality: Hands-On Practice*	*Assessment FOR Learning*
Chapter 5 How to write selected response test questions + student involvement	*Evaluating Assessment Quality* *Commonsense Paper and Pencil Assessments*	
Chapter 6 How to write extended response questions + student involvement	*Assessing Reasoning in the Classroom*	
Chapter 7 How to write performance assessments + student involvement	*Evaluating Assessment Quality* *Designing Performance Assessments* for *Learning*	*Creating & Recognizing Quality Rubrics*
Chapter 8 How to conduct assessment via personal communication + student involvement		

5

Part III: Communicating Assessment Results

CASL CHAPTER	VIDEO/DVD	RELATED BOOKS
Chapter 9 Overview of communication		
Chapter 10 Grading	*Grading & Reporting in Standards-Based Schools*	*Assessment FOR Learning* *Understanding School Assessment* *Creating & Recognizing Quality Rubrics* *A Repair Kit for Grading: 15 Fixes for Broken Grades*
Chapter 11 Portfolios		
Chapter 12 Student-involved conferences	*Student-Involved Conferences*	*Assessment FOR Learning* *Understanding School Assessment*
Chapter 13 Standardized tests		

5

References

Arter, J. A., & Chappuis, J. 2006. *Creating & recognizing quality rubrics*. Portland, OR: Educational Testing Service.

Black, P., & Wiliam, D. 1998. Inside the black box: Raising standards through classroom assessment. *Phi Delta Kappan, 80*(2), 139–148.

Chappuis, S., Stiggins, R. J., Arter, J. A., & Chappuis, J. 2005. *Assessment FOR learning: An action guide for school leaders*, 2nd ed. Portland, OR: Assessment Training Institute.

DuFour, R., Eaker, R., & DuFour, R. (Eds.). 2005. *On common ground: The power of professional learning communities*. Bloomington, IN: National Educational Service.

Guskey, T. 2000. *Evaluating professional development*. Thousand Oaks, CA: Corwin.

Lashway, L. 1998. Creating a learning organization. *ERIC Digest, 21*(April), n.p. Retrieved May 30, 2007 from http://chiron.valdosta.edu/whuitt/files/lrnorg.html

Lieberman, A. 1995. Practices that support teacher development. *Phi Delta Kappan, 76*(8), 591–596.

Murphy, C. U., & Lick, D. W. 2001. *Whole-faculty study groups: Creating student-based professional development*, 2nd ed. Thousand Oaks, CA: Corwin.

Sparks, D. 2000. Foreword. In Guskey, T., *Evaluating professional development* (pp. ix–xii). Thousand Oaks, CA: Corwin.

Sparks, D. 2005. Foreword. In Speck, M., & Knipe, C., *Why can't we get it right? Designing high-quality professional development for standards-based schools*, 2nd ed. (pp. ix–x). Thousand Oaks, CA: Corwin.

Sparks, D., & Hirsch, S. 1997. *A new vision for staff development*. Alexandria, VA: Association for Supervision and Curriculum Development.

Speck, M., & Knipe, C. 2005. *Why can't we get it right? Designing high-quality professional development for standards-based schools*, 2nd ed. Thousand Oaks, CA: Corwin.

Stiggins, R. J. 2006. Assessment for learning: A key to motivation and achievement. *EDge, 2*(2), 1–20.

Stiggins, R. J., & Chappuis, J. 2006. What a difference a word makes: Assessment FOR learning rather than assessment OF learning helps students succeed. *Journal of Staff Development, 27*(1), 10–14.